Thomas More
AND HIS UTOPIA
WITH A HISTORICAL INTRODUCTION

BY

KARL KAUTSKY

TRANSLATED BY

H. J. STENNING

INTERNATIONAL PUBLISHERS

NEW YORK   MCMXXVII

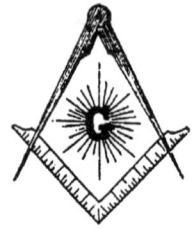

CONTENTS

PART I

THE AGE OF HUMANISM AND OF THE REFORMATION

CONTENTS

PART II

THOMAS MORE

PART III

UTOPIA

CHAPTER I

CHAPTER II

CHAPTER III

CHAPTER IV

CHAPTER V

Thomas More and His Utopia

PART I

THE AGE OF HUMANISM AND OF THE REFORMATION

INTRODUCTION

Two great figures loom on the threshold of Socialism: Thomas More and Thomas Münzer, two men whose fame rang throughout Europe in their lifetimes: one a statesman and scholar who attained to the highest position in his native land and whose works aroused the admiration of his contemporaries; the other an agitator and organiser, before whose quickly collected multitudes of proletarians and peasants the German princes trembled. Fundamentally different from each other in respect of standpoint, method, and temperament, both were alike as regards their object—communism, alike in daring and fidelity to conviction, and alike in the end which overtook them—both died on the scaffold.

It is sometimes debated whether the honour of having inaugurated the history of Socialism should fall to More or to Münzer, both of whom follow the long line of Socialists, from Lycurgus and Pythagorus to Plato, the Gracchi, Catilina, Christ, His apostles and disciples, who are sometimes mentioned in proof of the assertion that there have always been Socialists without the goal ever coming nearer.

We grant that with the development of commodity production a class of free persons without property arose in antiquity, who were called by the Romans proletarians. And in connection therewith endeavours to abolish or alleviate many social inequalities manifested themselves betimes. But the proletariat of old was quite different from the modern variety, and modern Socialism is equally different from antique Socialism.

There are historians who believe they find in the Rome of Julius Cæsar the same proletariat as in modern London, Paris, or Berlin. In reality, however, the modern proletariat has undergone manifold changes during the short space of 400 years it has existed, in accordance with concurrent economic development. The proletariat of to-day is markedly dissimilar from the proletariat of 1848, and much more numerous are its variations from its prototype in the days of *Utopia*, when Capital had but just entered on its economic revolution, and feudalism still wielded an extensive power over the economic life of the masses of the people.

The new ideas, prompted by the new interests, had not discarded the vestments of modes of thinking derived from feudalism, and the latter persisted as traditional illusions long after the main props of its material foundation had been knocked away.

The peculiar character of that time would necessarily colour the socialism which then arose. More was a child of his age; he could not overstep its limits, but it testifies to his perspicacity, and perhaps also to his instinct, that he already perceived the problems inherent in social development.

The bases of his socialism are modern, but they are overlaid by so much that is not modern that it is often extremely difficult to reveal them. While More's socialism is at no point reactionary in its tendency, inasmuch as he did not perceive the salvation of the world to lie in a return to feudal conditions, it frequently happened that only the resources of feudal times were at his disposal for solving the problems which confronted him. Consequently, he had to twist and turn them about in a truly fantastic manner to adapt them to his modern aims.

To the student who thoughtlessly examines More's communism many of his expedients will appear to be distorted, bizarre, and arbitrary, but they are, in fact, dictated by a thorough and well-digested knowledge of the needs and means of his time.

Like every other Socialist, More can only be understood in the light of his age, to comprehend which a knowledge of the beginnings of capitalism and the decline of feudalism, of the powerful part played by the Church on the one hand, and of world commerce on the other, is necessary. These influences had a profound effect upon More, and before we can sketch his personality and estimate his writings, it is incumbent on us to indicate, at least in outline, the historical situation whose product he was.

That is the task of the first part of our work.

CHAPTER I

THE RISE OF CAPITALISM AND OF THE MODERN STATE

1. *Feudalism.*

"THE sciences are flourishing and minds are active; it is a pleasure to be living," exclaimed Hutten of his time. And he was right. For joyfully combative spirits like his it was a pleasure to live in a century which boldly swept aside ancient conditions and inherited prejudices, which imparted fluidity to the inert social development and at one stroke infinitely extended the horizon of European society, which created new classes and released new ideas and struggles.

As a "Knight of the Spirit" Hutten had every reason to rejoice in his time. As a member of the Order of Chivalry he might have regarded it with less favourable eyes. The fate of his class was linked with that of the oppressed. Its alternative to extinction was to seek in servitude to a prince the livelihood which the soil refused to yield it.

The keynote of the sixteenth century is the death-grapple of feudalism with nascent capitalism. It bears the impress of both modes of production, and constitutes a strange mixture of the two.

The foundation of feudalism was peasant and handicraft production within the limits of the local community.

One or more villages formed a local community, with common property in woods, meadows, and water, originally in arable land too. Within this local community the whole process of medieval production went on. The common property in land, as well as the transmitted private property in fields and gardens, supplied the requisite means of life, the products of the cultivation of the fields, of cattle rearing, of hunting and fishing, and the raw materials which were worked up within the patriarchal peasant family or by the handicraftsmen of the village—wood, wool, etc.

Both private and public activity within this community aimed at supplying articles of use for consumption by the producer or his family or his community, or sometimes by the feudal lord.

A local community was an economic organism which was usually self-sufficing and had almost no economic contact with the outside world. This led to a remarkable exclusiveness. He who did not belong to the community was accounted a stranger, devoid of rights or possessing very few, even when he settled in the community, so long as he did not acquire a holding of land. The whole world outside the community was foreign. The members of the community developed, on the one hand, aristocratic pride towards newcomers from the world without, who were unable to acquire any landed property, and, on the other hand, that local narrowness, that parochial policy which may still be seen in remote and backward countries. Upon such foundations were based the particularism and the separation of castes peculiar to the feudal Middle Ages.

The economic ties of the feudal State were therefore extremely loose. Empires were rapidly formed and as rapidly fell to pieces. Even the national language did not form a tie of importance, as the exclusiveness of the local communities favoured the formation and maintenance of dialects.

The only strong organisation which stood above the

local communities was the universal Catholic Church, with her universal language, Latin, and her universal landed property. She it was who held together the entire mass of small, self-sufficing organisms of production in Western Europe.

The power of the Chief of State. of the King, was as slight as the ties of the State were loose. From the State itself the monarchy could derive but little power. It drew its strength, like every other social force of the time, from its landed property. The greater the landed property of a feudal lord, the more peasants in a community, the more communities in the country owing him fealty, the greater were his means of life, the greater in extent and variety were the personal services at his disposal; the larger and more splendid was the castle he could build, the more numerous were the handicraftsmen and artificers he could maintain at his Court, who supplied him with clothing, utensils, ornaments, and weapons; the larger was his travelling retinue, the more sumptuous his hospitality, the more vassals he could attach to himself.

The king was usually the largest landowner in the country, and therefore the most powerful. But he was not strong enough to impose subjection on the other land-owners. When united they were generally stronger than he, while the greatest among them was a formidable opponent. The king had to rest content with being recognised as the first among equals. His position became increasingly precarious as feudality developed, as the power of the feudal lords grew by the subjugation of free peasants, as the area from which a militia could be raised contracted, leaving the king dependent on an army of chivalry.

The national and local princely power generally began only to raise its head again when the towns were sufficiently consolidated to afford it a firm support.

2. *The Towns.*

The local community formed the basis of the medieval township as well as of the village. It was commerce, especially with Italy, which gave the impulse to its development. This commerce had never quite stopped after the downfall of the Roman Empire, even at the time of the greatest convulsions. The peasants, at any rate, did not require it, as they produced themselves what they needed. But the squires, the higher nobility, the higher clergy created a demand for the products of a higher industry. The artisans attached to their courts could only partially satisfy this need. They were not capable of producing fine linen, ornaments, and the like, such as Italy supplied. From time to time the German nobles procured these treasures during pilgrimages to Rome; but by the side of this a systematic commerce was growing up, which was especially sustained in Germany after the tenth century by the silver mining in the Harz district. The silver mines of Goslar began to be worked in 950.

At the courts of the secular lords, at the seats of the bishops, and at certain trade junctures, as where the roads from the Alpine passes touched the Rhine or the Danube, at protected places in the interior of the country, which were accessible to large ships, such as Paris and London, depôts for the warehousing of goods soon came into existence, which, insignificant as they may seem to us to-day, yet aroused the covetousness of the surrounding inhabitants and of foreign robbers, Normans, Hungarians, etc. It became necessary to fortify them. Thus a start was given to the development of the town from a village.

But even after the building of walls, agriculture and production for consumption within the limits of the local commune remained the chief occupation of the inhabitants of the fortified place. The commerce was too insignificant to alter its character. The town burghers remained as locally narrow and exclusive as the village peasants.

By the side of the old fully privileged families of the village community there arose in the meantime a new power, that of the artisans, who organised themselves in associations, in guilds, after the example of the commune.

Handicraft was not originally commodity production. The artisan stood in a certain relation of service either to the local commune, or, as a retainer, to a feudal lord. He produced for the needs of the local commune or of the Court to which he was attached, not for sale. Such artisans were, of course, very numerous in the towns, especially such as were the seats of bishops or the landed nobility. Other artisans were attracted as trade developed, and a market for the products of industry was opened. The artisan was now no longer obliged to work under a servile relationship. He could become a free producer of commodities. The servile artisans in the towns endeavoured to shake off their obligations, and those in the environs fled to the town when they thought it would protect them.

Handicraft grew apace; but it remained for the most part excluded from the local commune and consequently from the government of the town; the latter being reserved for the descendants of the original members of the village community, who developed from peasant communists into haughty patricians. A class struggle between the guilds and the old families set in, which generally ended with the complete victory of the former. At the same time a struggle was going on to procure the independence of the town from the overlordship of the landed or provincial nobility, and this independence was often achieved.

In these struggles with the landowning aristocracy the handicraftsmen felt a certain sympathy with the peasants, who were striving for an alleviation of their feudal burdens. Not infrequently both classes acted together.

A democratic and republican tendency among the lower burghers was fostered by these struggles, but it did not entirely abolish the earlier exclusiveness of the village community, which was merely extended to the guild and the municipality.

Handicraft commodity production at least broke down the exclusiveness of the urban community; the artisans worked not merely for the town, but also for the surrounding district, often serving an extensive area; not so much for the peasants, who continued to make for themselves almost all they needed, as for their exploiters, the feudal lords, who had lost the artisans attached to them. On the other hand, the artisans drew their means of life and raw materials from the country. The economic interactions, as well as the antagonism, between town and country began. By the side of the village community the town, with a larger or smaller vicinage, tended to increase in importance as a second economic unit. The segregation of the individual towns, persisted, however, despite their permanent or temporary association for common ends. The effect of this was to weaken, rather than strengthen, political cohesion, as the rich and proud city republic achieved an independence which would have been quite impossible for the village communities. They formed, by the side of the great feudal lords, a new occasion for political disruption.

With the aid of the towns, the power of the squires was directed against the nobility. Eventually, however, they were threatened with the fate of being completely destroyed by their former allies. But this tendency only asserted itself to a slight extent; for within the towns was growing up a new power which was to turn them into bulwarks of a rigid political absolutism: the revolutionary power of mercantile capital, which gave rise to world commerce.

3. *World Trade and Absolutism.*

As we already know, the trade between Italy and the
Teutonic North had never quite ceased, even after the fall
of the Roman domination.   It had founded the towns.
But it was too weak, so long as it remained chiefly petty
commerce, to impart to them a special character.   For
some time to come, agriculture within the confines of the
village communities, and later guild handicraft, occupied
most of their energies and determined their character.

This was the case with many towns until the last
century, and in some instances is even so to-day.   But
a number of townships grew into larger towns, and
thus became the pioneers of a new social order.   Such
were the towns which, owing to the special favour
of historical and geographical circumstances, became
centres for overseas trade, for world commerce.

In medieval Europe, the overseas trade with the East
first developed in Lower Italy, in Amalfi, where Greeks and
Saracens came into conflict with the natives and afterwards established trading relations with them.   Much as
the East had declined, it was infinitely superior to the
West in artistic skill and technical knowledge.   Not only
had the primeval branches of production been maintained
there, but new ones had grown up by their side, such as
the production and preparation of silk in the Greek Empire.
Moreover, the Islamic migration of peoples had brought
the highly civilised countries of the Far East, India and
China, into much closer contact with Egypt and the
seaboard countries of the Mediterranean than was the case
at the time of the Roman domination.

In the eyes of the European barbarians, the treasures
displayed by the merchants of Amalfi were valuable
beyond compare.   The greed to possess and acquire such
treasures soon seized all the ruling classes in Europe.

It powerfully contributed to those expeditions of plundering and conquest to the East which were known as the Crusades, but it also encouraged all the towns situated in a geographically favourable position to participate in such a lucrative commerce. First and foremost in North Italy.

In course of time attempts were made to imitate the products of industry which were imported, especially weaving. Even in the thirteenth century we find silk-weaving sheds in Palermo, operated by Greek prisoners of war. In the fourteenth century similar weaving sheds were established in the towns of North Italy.

Once the products were successfully imitated, the merchants soon found it more profitable to import the raw material and have it worked up at home by hired workers, provided they could find free workers, workers whom no guild compulsion or feudal service prevented from offering their services, and whom no ownership of means of production relieved from the necessity of selling their labour power.

In this way the arts of manufacture arose, and the foundations of the capitalist mode of production were laid.

In More's time, at the beginning of the sixteenth century, these beginnings were but faintly perceptible, and industry was still chiefly under the control of guild handicraft. Capital was mainly merchant's capital. But even in this form it was already exerting a disintegrating effect upon the feudal mode of production. The more the exchange of commodities developed, the greater became the power of money. Money was the commodity which everyone took and everyone needed, for which one could receive everything, everything which the feudal mode of production offered—personal services, house and hearth, food and drink—as well as innumerable articles which could not be produced under the family roof, articles the possession of which became increasingly necessary and which were not to be obtained except with money. The classes engaged in acquiring money, producing or exchanging, attained to increasing importance. The guildmaster who, owing to the legally restricted number of his journeymen, could only achieve moderate prosperity was soon outpaced by the merchant whose appetite for profit was boundless, whose capital was capable of unlimited expansion, and whose trading profits were enormous.

Merchant's capital is the revolutionary economic force of the fourteenth, fifteenth and sixteenth centuries. It revitalised society and provided men with fresh outlooks.

In the Middle Ages we find a narrow particularism, a parochial outlook side by side with a cosmopolitanism which comprised the whole of Western Christendom. The feeling of nationality was therefore very weak.

The merchant cannot confine himself to a small district as the peasant or artisan can. He wants the whole world in which to sell his goods. In contrast to the guild citizen, who may never pass beyond the walls of his town, we find the merchant untiring in his journeys to unknown countries. He passes beyond the boundaries of Europe, and inaugurates an epoch of discoveries which culminates in revealing the sea route to India and the discovery of America, and which, strictly speaking, is still going on to-day.

Even to-day it is the merchant who gives the impulse to most voyages of discovery, and not the scientific investigator. The Venetian Marco Polo got as far as China even in the thirteenth century. Ten years after Marco Polo, an attempt was made by daring Genoese to find a sea route to India by way of Africa, an undertaking which was to succeed two centuries later. Of greater significance for the economic development was the opening of direct sea communication from Italy to England and Holland, which was effected by Genoese and Venetians towards the end of the thirteenth century, and gave a strong impulse to capitalism in these countries of the North-West.

Commerce put in place of local ties a cosmopolitan feeling which was at home wherever a profit could be earned. At the same time it set up nationality against the universality of the Church. World trade widened the horizon of the Western peoples far beyond the region of the Catholic Church, and simultaneously narrowed it within the sphere of their own nation.

This sounds paradoxical, but it is easy to explain. The small, self-sufficing communities of the Middle Ages were scarcely, if at all, in economic antagonism with each other. Within these communities there were indeed antagonisms, but the outside world was regarded with indifference, provided it did not disturb the communities. For the great merchant, on the other hand, it is not a matter of indifference what relations the community to which he belongs has to the outside world. Trading profit arises from buying as cheap and selling as dear as possible. Profits largely depend upon the relative strength of buyers and sellers. It is, of course, most profitable to find oneself in the pleasant position of being able to take commodities from a commodity owner without giving him any return. In fact, in its beginnings, trade is very often indistinguishable from piracy. We see this in the Homeric poems, and we shall also see later that in the England of the sixteenth century piracy was a favourite form of the " primitive accumulation " of capital and therefore enjoyed State support.

With trade, however, competition arose among buyers as well as sellers. In the foreign market these antagonisms became national antagonisms. The conflict of interests, for example, between the Genoese buyers and the Greek sellers in Constantinople, became a national antagonism.

On the other hand, the conflict of interests between Genoese and Venetian merchants in the same market likewise became a national antagonism. The stronger Genoa was as compared both with Venice and the Greek Empire, the more trading privileges it might expect in Constantinople. The greater and more powerful was the homeland or the nation, the bigger were the profits.

The development of world trade therefore promoted a powerful economic interest, which tightened and consolidated the loose textures of States, but also brought about their separation from each other and divided Christendom into several sharply sundered nations.

After the rise of world-wide commerce home trade contributed equally to the strengthening of national States.

By its nature trade tends to concentrate in certain emporiums, junctions where the roads of a large district coalesce. There the goods from abroad are collected, in order to be distributed over the whole country by means of a complicated network of roads. At the same junctions the home commodities were collected in order to be despatched abroad. The whole district dominated by such an *entrepôt* became an economic organism, whose ties became all the closer, whose dependence upon the centre all the stronger, the more commodity production developed and supplanted production for use.

From all parts of the district dominated by this centre people flocked thence; some intending to remain there, others intending to return after the transaction of their business. The centre grew, it became a large town, in which was concentrated not only the economic life but also the intellectual life of the country which it dominated. The language of the town became the language of the merchants and of cultivated persons. It tended to supplant Latin and to become the written language. But it also began to supplant the peasant dialects; a national language came into existence.

Political administration was adapted to the economic organisation. This too was centralised, the political central power was installed at the centre of the economic life, and the latter became the capital of the country, which it now dominated not only economically but also politically.

In this way the economic development brought into being the modern State, the national state with a homogeneous language, a centralised administration, a capital.

This course of development was frequently distorted, but at the end of the fifteenth and beginning of the six- *end 15thc / beginning 16thc* teenth centuries its trend may be distinctly perceived in the States of Western Europe, and perhaps all the more distinctly because at the time feudalism still greatly influenced the economic life, and by the force of tradition to a still greater degree governed the forms of the intellectual life.   Assumptions taken for granted a few generations later had then still to assert their " right to existence " and likewise to impugn the ancient institutions. The new economic, political, and intellectual tendency had to cut a path through existing conditions; it had to enter upon controversy, and consequently its aim was often more sharply defined than in the following century.

It is noteworthy that the trend of development just described was bound to favour monarchy, or rather the power of the local prince, in all places where he had preserved a remnant of strength.   It was natural that the new political central power should cluster round the person of the local prince, and that he should form the head of the centralised administration and army.   His interests and the interests of commerce were the same.   The latter needed a reliable captain and a strong army, which, in accordance with the character of the economic power whose interests it served, was hired for money. Commerce needed the army to assert its interests both at home and abroad: to defeat competing nations, to conquer markets, to burst the bonds with which the small communities inside the State fettered free trade, to police the roads against the great and small feudal lords, who opposed a bold denial, not always of a theoretical nature, to the right of property which commerce proclaimed.

International intercourse also provided occasions for friction between the various nations. Commercial wars became more frequent and more violent. But every war increased the power of the princes and made them more and more absolute.

In the absence of a traditional princedom which this development would have favoured, a frequent result was the absolutism of the leaders of the mercenary hordes which the States required, as in various republics of Northern Italy.

But the new polity not only needed the prince as supreme captain. It also needed him as the chief of the political administration. The feudal administrative apparatus was in process of dissolution, the bureaucracy was as yet in its infancy. Political centralisation, which was an economic necessity for commodity production at the incipient stage of the capitalist mode of production, needed at the outset a personal head strong enough to maintain the unity of the administration against the discordant elements, especially the nobles.

This strength only the army captain possessed. The uniting of all the resources of the military and administrative apparatus on one hand, and princely absolutism on the other, was an economic necessity for the period of the Reformation and long afterwards. This cannot be emphasised sufficiently, as many of More's actions and writings must appear absurd from the modern standpoint, if we fail to take this point into consideration.

It seemed at that time hopeless, as in many cases it really was, to attempt to embark upon any political undertaking without or against the princes. Everything that happened in the State had to receive the sanction of the prince.

The stronger princely absolutism became in the State, the more it subserved the interest of Capital, then chiefly commerce and high finance. Not only were the interests of Capital and princedom up to a certain point identical, but princedom became more and more dependent on Capital.

The power of the princes ceased to rest upon their landed property in the degree that world commerce grew. Money tended to become the basis of this power, which was measured by the prince's army and the magnificence of his court. Both cost money. The feudal mode of warfare was supplanted by new and superior methods which the wealthy towns had developed. A rigidly disciplined infantry was opposed to the undisciplined army of chivalry. The new army's artillery also made it a formidable foe.

Consequently war became a question of money. Only those who had enough money to buy infantry, cannon, and large quantities of arms could indulge in the luxury of a war.

To this must be added the expense of the Court. The interests of commerce and of the monarchy alike required that the pride of the feudal noble should be broken. While his destruction was not desired, it was imperative that he should adapt himself to the new conditions. The noble must no longer linger in his stronghold supporting numerous retainers, who were useless, if not dangerous, for the monarchy and commerce.

2

The noble had to enter the king's service and remain at Court. Instead of spending his revenue upon the maintenance of his own armies, he was expected to dissipate it in luxury at Court, to spend it in purchasing just those commodities upon whose sale world commerce, the merchants' profits, depended. An English Act of Parliament passed in 1512, which regulated the duties on gold and silken stuffs, gold brocade, velvet damask satin, taffetas, and other materials woven out of silk and gold, mentions among other things, that 3,000 to 4,000 pieces of such cloth often came to England in one ship.

The Court luxury of the noble thus supported trade and monarchy in equal measure; it augmented profits and weakened the noble financially, making him dependent on money grants from the king and the credit of the merchants.

The merchant class and the monarchy at that time promoted the spread of luxury with all possible means, chiefly by their own example. Everything was done to attract the noble from his castle to the Court, if necessary by force, if possible by marks of honour and the enticements which refined luxury offered to rude simplicity.

Both monarchy and nobility moved in a circle of reciprocal emulation as regards the development of luxury.

At the beginning of the sixteenth century, property could not be invested in the funds or in shares. The idle rich who did not wish to engage in business as merchants, farmers, or manufacturers, above all the high nobility, invested their accumulated wealth in precious metals and precious stones, objects which always retained their value and found buyers everywhere. Gold and precious stones were then just such a power as a numerous retinue had been formerly. It was not enough to possess this power, it must be displayed. This was the best means to win influence which could command the subjection of some and the respect of others. The revenues of the feudal lords, which in the Middle Ages had been spent upon the upkeep of a numerous following, were now lavished upon valuables, and instead of appearing on festive occasions with their whole body of retainers, the nobles now appeared laden with all their jewels.

The king could not lag behind his courtiers; he also had to demonstrate the superiority of his power through his superior magnificence. Noble and monarch thus urged each other to ever more lavish displays.

Consequently from the fifteenth century onwards the maintenance of a splendid Court became a political need of increasing importance, without which a prince could not manage to exist. A senseless luxury developed, which swallowed up endless sums.

All this expenditure had for long exceeded the revenues derived by kings from feudal and landed property. They now began to levy money taxes, and looked to the wealthy towns, which were not to be trifled with, for most of this taxation.

The king was therefore often obliged to promise that no taxes would be imposed without the consent of the towns. The towns were summoned to send delegates, as the Third Estate, in order, in conjunction with the other two Estates, the nobility and the clergy, to agree with the king upon the amount of the taxes to be imposed. Where the towns had sufficient power, they would only consent to such taxes upon certain conditions. In England, under specially favourable conditions, brought about by the union of the small landowner with the burgher class, the legislative power of Parliament evolved out of this situation.

But the grants of money were rarely sufficient to stop up the holes made in the treasuries of the princes by ever-lasting wars and boundless court extravagance. Most princes were perpetually embarrassed despite the fact that the taxes oppressed the people most harshly. In this unpleasant predicament the rich commercial magnates and bankers were ready to help them, in return for pledging a portion of the State revenue. National debts were incurred, States and their leaders became debtors to Capital, whose interests they had to serve.

The power of absolutism grew as against the people. It overshadowed peasants and artisans, nobles and clergy. But absolutism clarified and defined the divergent outlooks and interests of commercial magnates, bankers, and land speculators.

The struggle of the eighteenth century, which led to the Great Revolution, turned essentially upon the question whether the monarchy should be a tool of the nobility and clergy or of the Third Estate. While the ideologists of the burgher class were acquainted with peasant and aristo- cratic republics, the idea of a middle-class republic occurred to scarcely one of them. The philosophers of the " En- lightenment " rather advocated an " enlightened " des- potism—that is, one conducted on their own lines. It was only the force of circumstances that imposed on the French a middle-class republic; this monarchy without a monarch did not become compatible with middle-class conditions until the mechanism of the centralised army and the bureaucracy was completely established and in working order.

CHAPTER II

LANDED PROPERTY

1. *Land Hunger—Feudal and Capitalist.*

COMMODITY production and the traffic in commodities not only created new classes with new interests and fresh outlooks, but also transformed the existing classes. The new needs to which they gave rise spread from the towns to the countryside, where they likewise evoked a desire for gold and silver, the commodities which would purchase anything. Thus it became necessary to adapt feudalism to the new conditions of production and make landed property a source of money; agriculture must be turned into commodity production; while the farmer might continue to produce for his own consumption, he was obliged, in addition, to raise a surplus to be brought to market as commodities.

This market was provided by the town, which needed not only foodstuffs, but also raw materials to an ever-increasing extent, not only corn and meat, cheese and butter, but also wool and flax, skins, wood, etc.

Under certain circumstances the peasant was able to become a commodity producer. Agriculture then became a source of money, and where this was the case, it lay in the power as well as in the interest of the peasant to convert into a money tax the personal service and the payments in kind which he was obliged to render to the feudal lord. Under specially favourable conditions he was even able to free himself entirely from the yoke of feudality.

Following the peasants' example, the feudal lords also strove to convert the feudal tributes into money taxes. But this conversion favoured the peasants only where conditions were unusually propitious. It proved disastrous for them where agricultural commodity production was not sufficiently developed. For the English peasants it was, at any rate, a means of loosening feudal ties; for the mass of German peasants money taxes became a scourge which drove them to despair and ruined them, without bringing the feudal lords any considerable advantage.

Meanwhile the English peasants did not have long to rejoice at their favourable situation. Commodity production imparted to the soil itself the character of a commodity and consequently a value which was not determined by the number of inhabitants it nourished, but by the surplus it yielded. The smaller the number of its cultivators in proportion to the yield, and the less pretentious their standard of life, the larger the surplus and the greater the land value.

We may therefore observe two peculiar phenomena throughout Western Europe at the close of the Middle Ages and the beginning of the new epoch: there arose a hunger for the land, especially for land which required few hands for its cultivation—e.g., forests and meadows. This was accompanied by an attempt to thin the agricultural population as much as possible, partly by substituting methods which required few hands for methods which required many, partly by adding to the labour burden of the individual cultivator, so that, for example, two persons would do what three persons did before.

The feudal epoch, too, knew land hunger as keen as that of the Renaissance; but its nature was entirely dissimilar. The old feudal lords were greedy for land *with* the peasants, the new lords wanted the land *of* the peasants.

What the feudal noble wanted was not land alone, but land and people. The more densely his land was populated, the greater the number of persons to pay taxes and render services, the larger was the military following which he could maintain. The efforts of the medieval noble was not directed to expelling the peasant, but to attaching him to the soil and attracting as many new settlers as possible.

The case was different with the new noble.

As the process of skinning the peasants did not yield enough money, he was more and more obliged to turn to commodity production, to establish his own agricultural undertakings—in England these were soon transferred to capitalist tenants. The peasants' land was required without its occupants, to expel whom every incentive existed.

Moreover, as already mentioned, value was imparted to meadows and forests. The feudal lords now began to treat as private property the common meadows and common forests, and to exclude the peasants from their use.

Now the sustenance of the peasant's livestock depended upon the commons. Horned cattle were not only useful to him on account of the milk, meat and tan they yielded, but they were indispensable to agriculture as draught cattle and manure suppliers. The forests were important for the peasant on account of the game and wood they furnished and as pasturage for pigs.

The peasant was therefore deprived of important means of industry when he lost the common forests and meadows, and at the same time he was ruined by the money taxes. Where the economic process of peasant expropriation did not proceed fast enough for the interest of the landlord, the latter often resorted to action on the basis of Roman law, which being unknown to the peasants, now suited the large landowners admirably, or even to direct physical force, without attempting any excuse.

Widespread impoverishment of the country people was the result of this development. The proletariat was further augmented by the dissolution of the monasteries, of which we shall speak in another connection, and the breaking up of the bands of retainers.

So long as no market existed for the products of agriculture, the landowners could not do anything with the large quantities of foodstuffs supplied by their bondsmen, except consume them, and as, despite their good stomachs, they could not do this alone, they invited others to help them, good friends, roving knights, travelling serfs, who were dependent on them, and lent them credit and power. The Earl of Warwick is said to have feasted 30,000 people in his castle on one day. He was powerful enough to make and unmake kings: he was the "king-maker."

All this changed when the landowners found an opportunity to sell the surplus of agricultural products which they could not consume, to exchange it for something which, under the new conditions, carried more respect and power than bands of retainers—*viz.*, money. Simultaneously the power of the princes grew, and with it the power of the police.

As internal feuds became rarer, retainers became increasingly superfluous. They began to appear to their masters as bands of idle gluttons, to be got rid of as far as possible. The princes assisted this process by compelling the dissolution of bands of retainers in those cases where they were a force which might be dangerous.

The break-up of the bands of retainers, the expulsion

of the peasants, and, since the Reformation, the dissolution of the monasteries, rapidly created an enormous mass of proletarians.

2. *The Proletariat.*

The Germanic peoples who invaded the Roman Empire were exposed to the possibility of impoverishment at the same time as they took over the Roman mode of production. In the time of the Merovingians we find among the beggars at the church doors mention of some with Frankish names. Throughout the Middle Ages the care of the poor was one of the most important functions of the Church. But poverty was still merely an isolated phenomenon. In the Middle Ages widespread distress was not unknown, but it was generally attributed to external enemies, or to nature: to forays of Hungarians or Normans, crop failures, etc. These distresses affected more or less the whole people, and were of a transitory nature. Not until the beginning of modern times did a proletariat again appear as a special and numerous class in society—a standing institution—as it had existed at the close of the Roman Republic and during the Imperial epoch.

But there was a great difference between the new and the antique proletariat. The new proletariat did not find a class beneath itself from whose direct or indirect exploitation it could have lived. Nor did the modern proletariat at the time of its rise possess any sovereign rights from the sale of which it could have derived profit, as did the sovereign populace of old Rome. The modern proletariat did not arise as the sediment of the ruling and exploiting classes; it was formed out of the dissolution of ruled and exploited classes. In the fifteenth century, for the first time in the history of the world, we see a class of free proletarians forming, as the lowest class in society, a class whose interests clamour not for the substitution of one class domination by another, but for the abolition of all class domination.

Only gradually did it become distinctly conscious of the fact that it was the lowest class in society. It could call nothing but its labour-power its own, and this it was obliged to sell if it was not to starve.

The new commodities were not long in finding buyers: captains and merchants. They were required in the mercenary armies and in manufactures. The impoverishment of the masses by the methods above indicated was as important for the development of war as of industry. But what capitalistic manufactures chiefly needed were skilled workers, which they found only rarely among the expelled peasants, soldiers, and monks. Handicraft did begin to supply proletarians—the guild masters were already complaining of the competition of the merchants who imported foreign commodities—but handicraft generally was still on a firm foundation. No wonder the capitalists bewailed the lack of workers, while the workers were wandering in thousands.

The wars absorbed large numbers of men, but the country folk were to a great extent rusty in the use of weapons, and from the close of the Middle Ages war became an art which had to be learnt. Not everyone could become a soldier, but he who did so remained a soldier and was incapable of any other trade. In the fifteenth and sixteenth centuries the standing armies were still very small, and most of the soldiers were discharged at the end of a war. Incapable of peaceful labour, demoralised and brutalised, the discharged soldiers frightened everyone; nobody would have anything to do with them. They became robbers, and naturally turned their attention to the most defenceless—the peasants. Themselves a consequence of the impoverishment of the masses, they became a means of accentuating this impoverishment. In Germany the impoverishment of the country population proceeded apace after the peasant war, while the development of capitalist industry and of a colonial policy was hindered by the change of world trade routes.

As the proletarians did not find in Germany the outlets that partly absorbed them in other countries, they were thrown back entirely on war and plunder. This would appear to be an important cause of the duration of the Thirty Years War. The war was possible because of the multitude of proletarians whence the armies were recruited. The war itself created fresh poverty among the peasants, and therefore produced new soldiers. The warring factions did not therefore find the reservoir of soldiers exhausted until the peasant had almost completely disappeared. Then to be sure there were no more soldiers.

Necessity obliged the workless who were unpractised in the use of arms to exploit the sympathy of the better situated. Vagrancy and swindling became a universal plague and robbers made all roads unsafe.

Vain was the attempt to suppress vagrancy by cruel and bloody laws, which did not provide opportunities for work or prevent the impoverishment of the country people. All efforts to protect the small peasant from the landowners proved fruitless. The poverty of the masses grew despite all laws and decrees.

3. Serfdom and Commodity Production.

The fate of the peasants left on the land was not much better than that of their liberated brothers. In many countries, especially in England, the peasant completely disappeared, to be replaced by the capitalistic farmer who employed day labourers, of which there was henceforth no lack.

Where the peasants were not supplanted by day labourers, they were reduced to the latter's level. In the Middle Ages the feudal lord needed his peasants. The more peasants he had, the greater was his power. When the towns were strong enough to protect absconding peasants against their lords, when the Crusades enticed away from the country a host of people who had become weary of the harsh yoke of serfdom, and the country began to be depopulated, the feudal lords were obliged to grant favourable conditions to retain their people and to attract others. This explains the improvement in the condition of the peasants in the thirteenth century. After the fourteenth century the feudal lords needed the peasants less and less, and their situation progressively worsened. The peasant homesteads were broken up in order to increase the area of the manor, and the peasant was often left with only a hut and a garden. The statute labour of the peasants was not correspondingly curtailed; on the contrary, it was prolonged indefinitely. Production for self-consumption had a certain limit, which was the needs of the persons to be supplied, even where it was based on forced labour, but commodity production with forced labour is marked by the same boundless greed for profit as is capitalism; of money one cannot have enough. Moreover, it encounters no obstacle such as the resistance which the free worker offers to capitalism.

Commodity production with forced labour is thus the most frightful of all forms of exploitation. Oriental patriarchal slavery seems an idyll compared with the slavery which prevailed in the sugar and cotton plantations of the Southern States not so many generations ago. And the serfdom of feudal times was incomparably milder than that which grew out of the development of commodity production.

The capitalist mode of production in the towns encouraged serfdom. Capitalism required for its develop-- ment wholesale importations of raw materials, which could then only be supplied by large-scale agriculture, operated by serfs. Serfdom in Europe was at certain times as much a vital condition for the capitalist mode of production as was later slavery in America.

As Marx wrote in 1847: " Direct slavery is the pivot of bourgeois industry. No cotton without slavery, no modern industry without cotton. Slavery alone gave the colonies their value; the colonies created world trade; and world trade is the basis of big industry " (*The Poverty of Philosophy*).

4. *The Economic Redundancy of the New Nobility.*

One result of the development of commodity production was that the forms of feudalism were utilised for the maximum exploitation of the agricultural worker, who could no longer be called a peasant.

While the serf was more intensely exploited, the feudal lord became increasingly superfluous. In the Middle Ages the feudal lord needed the peasant to maintain him, while the peasant needed the feudal lord, who protected him from violation, relieved him of part of his judicial and administrative duties towards the community, and above all freed him from the oppressive burden of military service.

One result of the development of the modern State was to weaken the causes which had robbed the peasant of his independence at the beginning of the Middle Ages. As the central political power was consolidated, and in- ternal feuds were suppressed, the nobles ceased to possess an independent military power, and the peasants ceased to require protection. The protecting lord now became the person from whom they required most protection.

The feudal lord had relieved the peasant of the burden of military service and taken it upon himself. The modern State shifted it from the feudal lord back to the peasant. The army of chivalry was replaced by a paid army, recruited from peasants. The maintenance of the army also fell on the peasants. Soldiers were quartered on him, and in addition to dues paid to the noble and the Church, taxes had to be paid to the State, chiefly for the maintenance of the army.

Although the noble continued to pride himself on being the country's chosen defender, his function consisted in filling the well-paid officers' posts.

To landed proprietorship, too, fell a diminishing share in administration and the dispensing of justice, which was more and more carried on by the bureaucracy, supported in part by additional taxes imposed on the peasants. What still survived of the old feudal justiciary in the patrimonial Courts became a new lever for exploitation.

Nothing remained of all the services which the noble once rendered the peasant, in return for equivalent services, while the duties of the peasants were indefinitely extended.

Eventually the feudal burdens and impediments became a real fetter on production. The feudal mode of appropriation came into conflict with the demands of the new mode of production. The feudal noble, long superfluous, from this point became decidedly harmful, and his removal was a necessity.

The peasant wars were, in effect, if not in form, the first violent protest against these beginnings of modernised feudalism adapted to the needs of commodity production, as above described. At the same time they were one of the last convulsions of the dying community, but they were also precursors of the Great Revolution of 1789.

5. *The Knighthood.*

Between the great nobles and the peasants stood the lesser nobility, the knights, who were descended from the old free peasants. While unable to escape feudal service to those above them, they were exempt from agrarian services and dues.

The knight stood between the large landed proprietor and the peasants, as to-day the lower middle class is between the capitalist and the worker, and he also played a similar equivocal part, to-day supporting the peasants and opposing the princes, and to-morrow reversing the *rôle* when the peasants became dangerous. The prototype of this class is Götz von Berlichingen. To be sure there were knights who whole-heartedly espoused the cause of the peasants, but most of them were unreliable: even Hutten's attitude towards the peasants was ambiguous.

Whether the knighthood espoused the cause of the peasants or that of the landowners, its downfall as an independent class could not be averted. Either the knight managed to climb into the class of large landowners, so extending his property as to be able to embark upon commodity production, or his estate became insignificant, often the prey of a powerful neighbour, always inadequate to support him according to the standard of his class. He was then obliged to disappear from the surface as a landowner and to seek his livelihood in the town as a merchant, or what counted as less derogatory, as a scholar in the retinue of a great lord—that is, as a kind of glorified lackey and bodyguard of the prince.

In Spain, England, and other countries, colonial policy offered a welcome opportunity to the lesser noble to realise his ideal: to become rich without working. The right of might conferred on him at home developed to a higher potency in the colonies and in piracy.

The adaptation of the lesser nobles to the new mode of production was, of course, no more effected without severe convulsions than were the other social transformations of the Reformation period. The knighthood strove obstinately to maintain its independence, which, however, was only possible if the feudal mode of production should survive in its original form. Moreover, the knighthood adopted the needs which the development of commodity production awakened among the ruling classes; the demands made by the knighthood upon life became greater as the possibility of satisfying them upon the basis of the feudal mode of production diminished.

The contrast between desires and capabilities in the knighthood became more and more pronounced and formed one of the peculiarities of the beginnings of the new age. The contrast often assumed a tragic form, but it did not seem so to urban literature which acclaimed the new money power. The knight, with the monk and the peasant, was the representative of the old feudal mode of production. Each of these three classes was hated and despised by the population of the great towns in which intellectual life was concentrated. But there was nothing hypocritical about the middle class while it was revolutionary, and moral indignation was the weapon it most rarely used. It fought its opponents with satire and mockery. The stupid peasant, the fat parson, the proud beggarly knight are among the favourite figures of the literature of the Renaissance and its offshoots.

We meet them first in Italy, where the new mode of production developed the earliest, but soon these figures were familiar in the literature of all Europe. From the *Decameron* (which appeared about 1352) of Boccaccio to *Don Quixote* (which appeared in 1604) there extended a long series of poems in which now the one, now the other, sometimes all three, of the aforesaid classes were held up to ridicule.

The greater part of this literature is now forgotten. Two figures among the many which formed the mocking epitaph of the knighthood are, however, still known to everybody: they are the immortal Don Quixote and Falstaff.

The *Merry Wives of Windsor* (written 1602) appears now to most readers as a very harmless comedy, but it typifies a bitter class struggle for all the rollicking humour which marks it. Whether Shakespeare pursued a political tendency in the comedy we do not know, but he described what he saw, the struggle between the decaying knighthood, which would not adapt itself to the bourgeois mould, and the aspiring middle class, whose women were wiser and braver than the knights without fear and reproach.

CHAPTER III

THE CHURCH

1. *The Church in the Middle Ages—Its Necessity and Power.*

THE class antagonisms indicated in the preceding chapter assumed the most various shapes in the course of their development, changing in accordance with time and place, and their elements combined according to external influences, historical traditions, and the interests of the moment, in the most manifold ways. But confused as the history of the fifteenth and sixteenth centuries may seem, a scarlet thread runs through it and stamps this age: the struggle against the Papal Church. The Church should not be confused with religion, with which we shall deal later.

The Church had been the predominant power in feudal times, and its fate was bound up with that of feudalism.

When the Teutons invaded the Roman world empire, they were confronted with the Church as the inheritor of the Cæsars, as the organisation which held the State together, as the representative of the mode of production of the dying epoch. Shrunken as this State was and retrogressive as was the mode of production, both were far superior to the political and economic conditions of the barbarous Teutons. The Teutons were superior morally and physically to decadent Rome, which, however, seduced them by its prosperity and its treasures.

Plundering is not a mode of production. The mere plundering of the Romans could not permanently satisfy the Teutons; they began to produce after the manner of the Romans. In the degree that they did so, they fell imperceptibly into dependence on the Church, which was their teacher, and when a political organisation corresponding to this mode of production became necessary, the Church alone could supply it.

The Church taught the Teutons improved methods of agriculture—the monasteries were model agricultural institutions until the late Middle Ages. It was also priests who taught the Teutons arts and handicrafts. Not only did the peasant thrive under the protection of the Church, but the Church also protected the majority of the towns until the latter were strong enough to protect themselves, and she encouraged trade.

The great markets were mostly held in or near churches. In every way the Church sought to attract buyers to such markets. She was also the sole power which in the Middle Ages attended to the maintenance of the great trade routes and facilitated travel by the hospitality of the monasteries. Many of the latter, as the hospices on the Alpine passes, were devoted almost exclusively to promote commercial intercourse. The Church deemed commercial intercourse so important that, in order to assist it, she allied herself with influences representing the culture of the late Roman Empire in the Teutonic States—*viz.*, Judaism, which the Popes protected for a long time. While the Germans remained unsophisticated Teutons, the Jews were cordially welcomed as the messengers of a higher civilisation.

The Teutonic Christian merchants did not become Jew baiters until they understood huckstering equally as well as the Jews.

That all the knowledge of the Middle Ages was to be

found in the Church, that she supplied builders, engineers, doctors, historians, and diplomats, is well known.

Tho whole material life of mankind, as well as its mental life, was an outflow from the Church: no wonder she captured the whole of mankind, and determined how men should think and feel. Not only did birth, marriage, and death give her occasion for intervention, but also labour and the festivals were regulated and controlled by her.

Moreover, the economic development made the Church necessary not only for the individual and the family, but also for the State.

We have already pointed out that when the Teutons moved to a higher mode of production, to developed agriculture and urban handicraft, a new political system became necessary.

But the transition to a new mode of production proceeded too rapidly, especially in the Romance countries, Italy, Spain, and Gaul, where it was already rooted in the native population, to permit the Teutons to fashion the new political organ out of their primeval constitution. Political functions devolved almost wholly upon the Church, which had become a political organisation in the late Roman Empire.

The Church made monarchs of the Teutonic chiefs, who had been democratic popular leaders and captains; but as the power of the monarch grew over the people, so did the power of the Church over the monarch. He became her puppet, and the Church became mistress instead of teacher.

The medieval Church was essentially a political organisation. Its extension signified the extension of the political power. The establishment of a bishopric in a heathen country by a monarch did not merely signify a campaign for the conversion of the heathen; for such an object neither Charles the Great would have ruined the Frankish peasants and slain innumerable Saxons, nor would the Saxons, tolerant in matters of faith, have offered an obstinate resistance to Christianity for decades. The establishment of a bishopric in a heathen country meant the grafting of the Roman mode of production on to the country where the bishopric was established.

The nearer the Teutons came to the social level of the Roman Empire at the time of its fall, the more necessary the Church became both for State and people. While she was useful for both, her own interests were not neglected. The services she rendered were dearly bought; the only general tax known to the Middle Ages, the tithe, flowed into her coffers.

The most important source of power and revenue in the Middle Ages was, however, landed property. The Church developed the same hunger for land and people as the nobility, and, like the latter, sought to acquire land and gain subjects. The landed property which the Church had possessed in the Roman Empire was mostly abandoned to her by the Teutonic invaders; where this was not the case she was soon able to regain it and something in addition. As the Church offered as much protection as the nobles, many peasants came under her sway. The Church conducted the political administration and priests were the counsellors of kings. It is not surprising that they were often prevailed upon to bestow Crown lands upon the Church. In conquered heathen countries the ample equipment of monasteries and bishoprics was dictated by necessity.

Meanwhile the Church was the sole power on which the king could rely in contests with the nobility. The best way to weaken an arrogant noble was to deprive him of a portion of his land and give or lend it to the Church.

Sometimes the Church did not wait until peasants, kings

and nobles were disposed to add to her property; she took what she could and, when called to account, justified the theft by a forged deed of gift. Reading and writing were almost a monopoly of the priesthood. In the Middle Ages forged deeds were as customary a means to legalise the acquirement of lands as are to-day mortgages, executions, and the like.

It looked as if the Church aspired to become the sole landed proprietor in Christendom. But the mightiest were to be curbed in their pride. The nobles were always hostile to the Church; when the latter acquired too much land, the king turned to the nobles for assistance in setting limits to the pretensions of the Church. Moreover, the Church was weakened by the invasion of Heathen tribes and the Mohammedans.

In view of the fluctuations to which the property of the Church was subject, it is difficult to estimate its extent in an age that had no idea of statistical measurements. Speaking generally, it may be said that in the Middle Ages one-third of the land was in the hands of the Church.

We have indicated what power was conferred by landed property in the Middle Ages. This applied with special force to the Church. As her properties were the best cultivated, the most thickly populated, her towns the most flourishing, the revenue and the power which she derived from them was greater than what a property of equal extent afforded the nobility or the monarchy. But as this income was mostly paid in kind, the problem was how to dispose of it. The monks and clergy could not consume it all. Although the abbots and bishops of the Middle Ages carried on feuds, like secular lords, the Church was seldom sufficiently bellicose to consume most of her revenues in fighting. Her advantage lay in her intellectual rather than her physical superiority, and her economic and political indispensability. She had less to expend on warlike aims than the nobility, while her income was greater. Her landed property was not only the most fertile, but she was entitled to a tithe from the land not subject to her.

She had therefore less reason than the nobles to exploit her subjects, to whom she was usually benevolent.

It was pleasant to live under the Cross ; at any rate, better than under the sword of noble lord keen on war and hunting. Despite this relative forbearance, a super-fluity of the means of life remained to the various ecclesiastical institutions, which the latter had no use for except to relieve the poor.

Here, as in many other points, the Church was only continuing her traditions from the imperial age. In the decaying Roman Empire pauperism was always increasing, and the relief of the poor became a problem of growing complexity for the State.

But the old Pagan State was not able to solve it, and relief of the destitute was undertaken by the new organisation created by the altered conditions, the Church.

It became one of her most important functions, to which she was not a little indebted for the rapid growth of her power and her wealth. The philanthropic institutions of private persons, of municipalities, of the State itself, which became more and more necessary and expensive, were handed over to the priests for administration. It is easy to understand why the influence of the Church over the whole people steadily increased.

The object of the gifts to the Church, as well as of the regular dues, was largely to assist the relief of the poor. In the case of tithes, it was laid down that they were to be divided into four parts :one for the bishop, one for the lower clergy, one for public worship, and one for the maintenance of the poor.

As the Teutons adopted the Roman mode of production, the inevitable result followed—private property and poverty. Common property in wood and meadows and untilled ground, which still survived by the side of private property in cultivated land, checked the impoverishment of the peasant. But in the early Middle Ages events frequently happened which plunged whole districts into distress and poverty. To the eternal wars and feuds of the lords were added invasions of nomadic tribes or raids of pirates, such as Normans, Hungarians, and Saracens, which were so disastrous for settled agrarian peoples. Failures of the crops were also a frequent cause of distress.

When the distress was not so acute as to bring ruin upon the Church, the latter was the angel of salvation. She opened the great granaries in which her reserves were stored, and succoured the needy. And the monasteries were great almshouses, which afforded refuge to many a decayed and impoverished noble, driven from hearth and home or disinherited. By entering the Church he attained power, repute, and prosperity.

There was no class in feudal society which did not have an interest in supporting the Church—although not to the same extent. To question the existence of the Church in the Middle Ages was to question the existence of society and of mankind. To be sure the Church conducted violent struggles with other classes, but in these her existence was not at stake, it was a question of degrees of power. The whole of material and, likewise, mental life was dominated by the Church which was interwoven with the whole life of the people, until in the course of time the ecclesiastical mode of thinking became a kind of instinct blindly followed, like a natural law, and to act contrary to it was felt to be unnatural. All expressions of political, social, and family life were clothed in ecclesiastical forms. And the forms of ecclesiastical thinking and behaving persisted long after the disappearance of the material causes which had produced them.

It was natural that the power of the medieval Church should develop the earliest in the countries which had formerly belonged to the Roman Empire—in Italy, France, Spain, England, later in Germany, and latest in the North and the East of Europe.

The German tribes, which during the migration of peoples had sought, in opposition to the Roman Church, to establish their States on the ruins of the Roman Empire, an antagonism which was expressed by their adhesion to the Arian sect, either vanished like the Ostrogoths and Vandals, or escaped impending downfall by submitting to the Roman Church.

But predominance in Western Europe fell to the tribe which at the outset had founded its empire in alliance with the Church of Rome, the tribe of the Franks.

The King of the Franks, in alliance with the head of the Roman Church, established the union of Western Christianity as an organism with two heads, a secular and a spiritual. It was a union against enemies pressing from all sides, and was imperatively dictated by the conditions.

But neither the King of the Franks nor his Saxon successors could make this union permanent. The Roman Popes accomplished what the Roman Emperor of the German nation had vainly attempted, the gathering of Christendom under a single monarch.

No feudal king, whatever his race, could perform this task, which required an organisation stronger than the monarchy—*viz.*, the centralised Church.

2. *The Basis of the Papacy's Power.*

Even before the migration of peoples the Bishop of Rome was the head of the Western Church; he was the heir of the Roman Emperor, as representing the city which had always been the actual capital of the Western Empire, although it had ceased to be the residence of the Emperor.

The break-up of the Roman Empire was accompanied by a temporary eclipse in the power of the Popes of Rome, and the ecclesiastical organisations of the various Teutonic Empires became independent of them. But the Popes quickly regained their former position, and even strengthened it. However decayed Italy might be, she was always the most highly cultivated country in Western Europe. The level of agriculture there was higher than in any other country. Industry was not quite extinct, and there was still some small trade with the East. The treasures, and also the mode of production, of Italy were the envy of the semi-barbarians beyond the Alps. The closer their tie with Italy, the more prosperous they became. The powers which had a special interest in this development, because they benefited from it—the monarchy and the Church in every Christian country of the Occident— aimed at strengthening the ties with Italy. But Italy's centre was Rome. The more dependent on Italy in an economic respect the Western countries became, the more dependent became their kings and bishops upon Rome, and the more the centre of Italy became the centre of Western Christendom.

The economic dependence of Italy and the influence of Rome upon Italy (so far as this obtained in the realm of Catholicism and not of the Greek Church and of Islam) were then scarcely so preponderating as to explain the enormous power which the Papacy obtained. These factors merely explain why the direction of Christendom fell to the Popes. But the tendency was for mere advice to become commands. When struggles broke out which threatened the whole of Christendom, the Papacy, being the sole influence recognised by all peoples as their leader, inevitably assumed the leadership and organised the resistance. The longer the struggles lasted and the greater their extent, the more the directive power became absolute master, the more it enlisted in its service all the forces mustered against the common enemy.

And such struggles came. The collapse of the Roman Empire set in motion not only the Teutons, but also all the numerous, apparently inexhaustible, tribes of semi-barbarians in the neighbourhood. As the Teutons moved towards the West and South, other peoples pressed upon them. The Slavs crossed the Elbe; from the steppes of South Russia came one Cossack tribe after another, as well as Huns, Avarians, and Hungarians (the latter at the end of the ninth century), who extended their plundering expeditions along the unprotected Danube, and even beyond the Black Forest and the Rhine, and beyond the Alps to Northern Italy. From Scandinavia, too, expeditions of Norman pirates followed one another. No sea was too broad for them to traverse, no empire too large to attack. They ruled the Baltic, seized Russia, established themselves in Iceland, discovered America long before Columbus; but what for us is important, from the end of the eighth to the twelfth century, they threatened to destroy the whole laboriously constructed civilisation of the settled Teutonic tribes. Not only were the coastwise countries of the North Sea entirely devastated by their plundering expeditions; with their small ships they sailed up the rivers and penetrated far into the country; nor did they fear the dangers of a long sea voyage. They soon began to attack the Spaniards, and finally extended their raids as far as Southern France and Italy.

The most dangerous enemy of the settled Teutonic tribes was, however, the Arabs, or rather the Saracens, as the writers of the Middle Ages called all those Eastern peoples set in motion by the Arabs to seek booty and a habitat in more highly civilised countries. This, of course, did not prevent the Saracens from absorbing this civilisation in the course of time and propagating it.

In the year 638 the Arabs invaded Egypt, and quickly conquered the whole of the Northern Coast of Africa; they appeared at the beginning of the eighth century in Spain, and not quite a hundred years after their invasion of Egypt, they threatened France. Charles Martel's victory saved France from the fate of the Empire of the Western Goths; but the Saracens were by no means rendered powerless.

They stayed in Spain, established themselves in Southern Italy and at various points of North Italy and Southern France, occupied the most important Alpine passes, and sallied forth to raid the northern slopes of the Alps.

During the migration of peoples the settled Teutonic tribes had occupied the greater part of Europe and a part of North Africa; now they saw themselves confined to a small space, and were hardly able to maintain this. Burgundy, which was practically the geographical centre of the Catholic West in the tenth century, was as much exposed to the invasions of the Normans as to that of the Hungarians and Saracens. The end of the peoples of Western Christendom seemed at hand.

And just when the pressure of external foes was most severe, the political power was most impotent, the feudal anarchy was most unchecked, and the only firm, coherent power was the Papal Church.

Like the monarchical powers, the Papal power, in its

contest with the external enemy, became strong enough to defy its foes at home.

The Saracens, who were to some extent superior in culture, could only be grappled with by the sword; in the fight with Islam the Papacy summoned and organised the whole of Christendom. The unstable enemies in the North and East could be temporarily repulsed by force of arms, but not permanently subdued. They were subjugated by the same means as the Roman Church had employed to subjugate the Teutons: they were forced to adopt a higher mode of production—after being won for Christianity, they settled down and were rendered harmless.

The Papacy celebrated a brilliant triumph over the Normans. It transformed them from the most formidable of the Northern enemies of Christianity into the most pugnacious and energetic antagonists of the Southern enemy. The Papacy made an alliance with the Normans similar to that which it once concluded with the Franks. The alliance recognised the fact that the Normans had not been pacified by their incorporation in the feudal mode of production. They remained a restless, predatory people, but the object of their raids was now changed. By being made feudal lords, the land hunger peculiar to feudalism was aroused in them, and from plunderers they became conquerors.

The Papacy knew how to make excellent use of this appetite for conquest—by turning it against the Saracens. The Papacy had as much to gain from the victory of the Normans as the Normans from the victory of the Papacy. The Normans became vassals of the Pope, who invested them with their conquests as fiefs. The Pope blessed their arms, and the Papal blessing was of great effect in the eleventh century, as it placed the powerful organisation of the Church at the service of the recipient. With Papal assistance the Normans were enabled to conquer England and Lower Italy.

By enlisting the Normans in its service, the Papacy attained to the summit of its power. It triumphed not only over its internal enemies, it not only imposed on the German Emperor the humiliation of Canossa; it felt strong enough to take the offensive against the Saracens: the epoch of the Crusades began.

The Popes were the organisers of the Crusades, the Normans their champions. What drew the latter towards the East was land hunger; they established feudal States in Palestine, Syria, Asia Minor, Cyprus, and finally in the Greek Empire as well.

Next to the Normans the majority of the Crusaders was composed of people for whom social pressure at home had become intolerable, serfs excessively exploited by their feudal lords, lesser nobles crushed by the preponderance of the great feudal lords.

In the chivalric army of the first Crusade the Normans were most conspicuous. The peasant army was characteristically commanded by several decayed knights, of whom one bore the expressive name of " Walter the Penniless." In the thriving East they hoped to obtain what their country denied them: well-being and prosperity.

It testifies to the great power of the Papacy that it was able to compel many elements to participate in the Crusades which had nothing to gain thereby. Many German emperors were obliged, much against their will, to recruit for the Papal armies and to carry the Papal flag, the Cross.

3. *The Overthrow of the Papal Power.*

The Crusades marked the highest point of the Papal power. They were a powerful agent in promoting the rapid development of the element that was destined to overthrow the feudal world and its monarch, the Pope. We mean Capital.

Through them the East was drawn closer to the West, commodity production and trade were alike promoted. The Church then began to wear an altered countenance. The development of landed property as a result of the growth of rural commodity production reacted in various ways upon ecclesiastical landed property. Additional burdens were placed on the peasants, common land was annexed, and farms were broken up.

Growing avarice impelled the Church to practise increasing parsimony in the relief of the poor. What had once been given gladly because it could not be consumed, was now retained because it had become a saleable commodity, because it could be exchanged for money, wherewith articles of luxury could be purchased. The fact that laws were passed with the object of compelling the Church to support the poor proves that she no longer met her obligations in an adequate manner. In the reign of Richard II. of England a law was passed (1391) ordering the monasteries to devote a portion of the tithes to the support of the poor and the lower clergy.

While the Church aroused the bitterness of the humble people because she afforded them too little protection against impoverishment, she drew on herself the enmity of the burgher class, because she still formed a certain bulwark against the impoverishment of the masses, as this process was not proceeding fast enough. The propertyless person was not delivered bound hand and foot to Capital so long as he received even scanty alms from the Church. That the monks were allowed to live an idle life instead of being thrown on the streets and placed at the capitalist's disposal as wage slaves, was in the eyes of aspiring burgherdom a sin against the national welfare.

That the Church should still keep the numerous festivals of the feudal times, despite the maxim of nascent burgher society that the workers do not work to live, but live in order to work, was nothing short of a crime.

The increasing wealth of the Church aroused the envy and the avarice of all the propertied classes, especially the great landowners and the land speculators. Even the kings thirsted for ecclesiastical treasures, in order to fill their coffers and buy " friends."

In the measure that the avarice and wealth of the Church grew as a result of the spread of commodity production, in the same measure she became superfluous in economic and political respects. In the towns a new mode of production had developed, which was superior to the feudal mode, and the towns supplied the organisations and the men which the new society and the new State needed. The priests ceased more and more to be teachers of the people, the knowledge of the population, especially in the towns, advanced beyond them, and they became one of the most ignorant sections of the people.

Moreover, the Church tended to become superfluous in connection with political administration. The modern State at least required the parish priests in the country; even to-day the parish priests have administrative functions, albeit of a trivial nature, to fulfil in backward countries.

Only when the modern bureaucracy was highly developed could the complete abolition of the parish priests as a political institution be contemplated.

The parish clergy were still necessary in the sixteenth century; nobody thought of abolishing them; but the modern monarchy, based upon financial power, no longer needed to be subservient to them or their leaders, the bishops.   The priests were obliged to become State officials, so far as they were necessary for political administration.

Two elements of the Church, however, tended to become increasingly superfluous and even an obstacle from an economic and political standpoint, two elements which had been of prime importance in the Middle Ages: the monasteries and the Papacy.

The former became superfluous for the peasants, like every feudal lord; superfluous as protectors of the poor; superfluous as guardians of the arts and sciences, which were thriving in the towns; superfluous for the cohesion and administration of the State; and finally they became superfluous owing to the obsolescence of the Papacy, whose strongest support they had been.

Without any functions in social and political life, ignorant, idle, rude, albeit immensely rich, the monks sank deeper and deeper into vulgarity and dissipation, and became a subject of universal ridicule. Boccaccio's *Decameron* shows us better than the most erudite treatise the demoralisation of monkery in the fourteenth century in Italy. In the following century matters were no better. The extension of commodity production propagated the moral infection of the monasteries as far as Germany and England.

The Papal power became as superfluous as the monasteries. Its chief function, the union of Christendom against the infidel, disappeared with the success of the Crusades. True the adventurers from the West could not maintain their conquests in the countries of Islam and of the Greek Church. But the power of the Saracens was none the less broken. They were driven from Spain and Italy and ceased to form a danger for the West.

Instead of the Arabs and the Seljuks, a new Oriental power arose, the Osmans, who destroyed the Greek Empire and threatened the West. But the attack this

4

time came from another side, not from the South, but
from the East; it hurled its weight not against Italy, but
against the Danubian countries.

The attack of the Saracens had threatened the very
existence of the Papacy, which was obliged for its own
preservation to summon the forces of the whole of Christendom against the infidels. From the Turks, however,
the Papal territories had little to fear, so long as the
Venetians and Knights of St. John resisted them in the
open harbours of the Mediterranean. The Hungarians
were the first to be attacked by the Turks, after the latter
had crushed the South Slavs, and then it was the turn of
South Germany and Poland. The struggle against the
Turks was not the business of the whole of Christendom,
but a local affair pertaining to its eastern bulwarks. As
the struggle against the Heathens and Saracens had
fused the whole of Christendom into the Papal monarchy,
so the struggle against the Turks now united into one
polity the Hungarians, Czechs, and South-Eastern
Germans, and the Hapsburg Monarchy came into
existence.

Towards the end of the fourteenth century the Turks
began their raids on Hungary, and caused Sigismund,
the king of that country, to march against them. He
suffered a terrific defeat at Nikopolis in the year 1396.
A second defeat, equally severe, was inflicted on the Poles
and Hungarians under King Ladislaus at Varna (1444).
In 1453 Constantinople fell into the hands of the Turks.
The Turkish danger flared up.

For a period the Papacy held fast to its traditions,
although they were becoming increasingly meaningless,
and acted as if it intended to perform the task of organising
the opposition against the Turks. But its zeal tended to
diminish, and the resources which the Popes collected from
the peoples of Christendom for the struggle against the

Turks were to an increasing extent diverted to the private use of the Popes themselves. The power of the Papacy and belief in its mission, which up till the twelfth century had been instruments for saving the peoples of Christendom, after the fourteenth century became instruments for their exploitation.

The centralisation of the Church had placed her resources wholly at the service of the Papacy, whose power was thereby enormously increased, but whose wealth was but slightly augmented so long as commodity production still remained weak and undeveloped. So long as the greater part of the revenues of the Church were paid in kind, the Papacy could not derive any considerable advantage from them.

The princes or bishops could not send corn, meat, and milk across the Alps. But money was a rarity until far into the period of the Crusades. In any case, as its power grew, the Papacy obtained the right of filling ecclesiastical offices outside Italy, and thus made the clergy dependent upon it. But so long as social or political functions were connected with these posts and the greater part of their revenues were paid in kind, they had to be filled by men willing to work, acquainted with the country, and prepared to remain there. The Pope could neither fill them with his Italian favourites nor sell them.

All this changed with the development of commodity production. Church, princes, and people were now able to obtain money. Money is easily transportable, does not lose its value on the way, and may be spent quite as well in Italy as in Germany.

This gave an impetus to the tendency of the Papacy to exploit Christendom. Like every other class the Papacy had striven to derive the utmost advantage from its social utility. Consequently, as its power grew, it sought to impose money taxes upon the ecclesiastical organisations and the lay world, and this money it required to enable it to perform its functions.   But, as stated, these money dues were originally insignificant.   As commodity production extended, the Popes became more avaricious and intensified their exploitation of the lay world, while their functions became less and less important.

The Popes of the fourteenth, fifteenth, and sixteenth centuries were as inventive as modern financiers.   The direct taxes imposed were usually small.   The Peter's Pence collected from the Poles in 1320 could scarcely have yielded much.   A higher sum was yielded by the Peter's Pence which had been sent to Rome from England ever since the eighth century.   Small at the beginning— it served to support a college for English priests in Rome— this tribute had increased so much by the fourteenth century as to surpass the income of the English king.

But, like other financial geniuses, the Papacy preferred indirect to direct taxes, which disclosed the exploitation too plainly.   Trade was then the chief means of cheating people and acquiring great wealth quickly.   Why, then, should not the Popes also become traders dealing in the commodities which came cheapest to them ?   The commerce in ecclesiastical posts and indulgences began.

In fact, ecclesiastical offices became very valuable commodities in the course of the development of commodity production.   A number of the Church's functions either disappeared or became obsolete.   But the offices which were established to execute these functions remained, and were often augmented.   Their revenues grew with the power and avarice of the Church, and an increasing portion of these revenues were paid in cash and could be consumed elsewhere than in the place to which the office was attached.   Thus a number of ecclesiastical offices became mere sources of revenue, and value was imparted to them as such.

The Popes presented them to their favourites or sold them, mostly, of course, to Italians and Frenchmen, who had no idea of filling the posts, especially if they were in Germany and their stipends could be sent across the Alps.

Moreover, the Church devised other means for exploiting the ecclesiastical positions; in particular, the annates, fines which every newly installed bishop paid to the Papal Stool.

In addition, there was the traffic in pardoning sins, which became ever more shameless.

The indulgences followed one after another (we find five indulgences shortly before the Reformation: 1500, 1501, 1504, 1509, 1517); their sale was eventually even farmed out.

The revolt against the Papacy was essentially a struggle between exploiters and exploited, not a struggle over mere ecclesiastical dogmas or vague slogans, such as a struggle between " authority " and " individualism."

The Popes hastened their own destruction by becoming increasingly contemptible. This is the fate of every ruling class that has become obsolete and is approaching extinction. Their functions dwindle as their wealth grows, and nothing remains for them to do but dissipate the proceeds of their extortions.

They decline intellectually and morally, often physically too. In the degree that their senseless extravagance provokes the famished multitude, they lose the strength to maintain their rule. Thus sooner or later every class is removed that has become injurious to society.

As we already know, Italy was the richest country in Western Europe during the Middle Ages; she preserved most of the traditions of the Roman mode of production; she was the medium for trade between East and West; commodity production and capitalism first developed in Italy.

It was there that a new outlook on life, hostile to

the ecclesiastical-feudal, first arose. With the headlong arrogance of youth, the burgherdom thrust aside all traditions, discipline, and morality. The Popes could not escape the influence of their environment. In fact, as secular princes of Italy, they marched at the head of the new revolutionary mental tendency. As such they pursued the same policy as all the other princes of their time, encouraging the middle class and fostering trade and national greatness. As heads of the Church, on the other hand, their basis was international and they were obliged to cling to the foundation of the ecclesiastical power, the feudal mode of production. Revolutionary in their secular capacity, they were reactionary in their ecclesiastical capacity. We therefore find in the Popes of the fifteenth and early sixteenth centuries a peculiar mixture of two very diverse elements, youthful daring and senile lasciviousness. The revolutionary contempt for the traditional, proper to an aspiring class, mingles with the unnatural sensuality of an exploiting class hastening to its destruction.

This strange combination of opposites interpenetrates the whole mental life of the Italian Renaissance. The mixture of revolutionary and reactionary elements was a feature of Humanism and distinguished the Humanist Thomas More.

Revolutionary or reactionary, the result was a life which violated all feudal conceptions of property and morality. And this dissolute mode of life achieved its acme while Germany was yet living under the ban of feudalism.

Prior to the Reformation it was a custom to make a pilgrimage to Rome. Three things, says Hutten, brought the pilgrim back: a bad conscience, a queasy stomach, and an empty purse.

It may be imagined that the picture which such a

pilgrim drew of the Holy Father would hardly correspond to the medieval ideas of sanctity. More shocking for pious souls, however, was the unbelief that prevailed in Rome and which the Pope scarcely concealed.

Sceptical as the Popes and their courtiers might be, they did not lose sight of the fact that faith was the basis of their power. After the material conditions had disappeared which had made the Popes masters of Christendom, the ideas springing from the conditions remained as their sole support, and these ideas came ever more into conflict with the social facts. The power of the Papal Church depended upon keeping the people ignorant of these facts, deceiving them, and hindering their development in every way. While this motive might be present only to a few thoughtful members of the Church, the priests everywhere fostered the credulity of the people in order to extract money from them. A swindling traffic in miraculous pictures and relics began. The zeal of the various churches and monasteries to impute the greatest miracles to their relics was one of the first expressions of free competition.

With competition came the tyranny of fashion. The priests must continually invent new saints to attract the multitude by the charm of novelty.

The greater the scepticism of the Papacy became, the more zealously it encouraged superstition, giving offence to the pious by the former and to the free-thinking by the latter.

Indignation at immorality, scepticism and superstition would have been ineffectual, had not the Papacy become a mere exploiting machine. It had already fallen into a dubious moral state before it reached the summit of its power. It was the economic and political, not the moral changes, which impelled the peoples to break away from the Papacy.

In many countries, especially in Germany, all classes had an interest in ending the connection with the Papacy; not alone the exploited people, but also the native exploiters, who were enraged at seeing so much money leave the country. Even the national clergy had an interest in the separation of the Church. In fact, they were merely the tax gatherers of the Roman Stool; they had to send to Rome the lion's share of what they collected from the people; the fattest benefices they had to yield to Rome's favourites, while the badly paid and onerous curacies were left to them. It was precisely that section of the clergy which still performed certain functions in the life of the State, which continued to enjoy a certain repute among the people, the secular clergy, that was impelled by its interests to offer the most energetic opposition to the Roman Stool.

The centralisation of the Church had not been an easy task for the Popes, but had been imposed in the course of violent struggles upon the ecclesiastical organisations of the individual countries. The various orders of monks had proved an effective tool for the subjugation of the secular clergy. As early as the eleventh century there were hostile relations between the Pope and the German bishops. The latter supported Henry IV., while the higher nobility espoused the Papal cause. Only after severe struggles were even the French and English Churches made to submit to the Papal supremacy.

The struggle between Rome and the various national churches did not, however, entirely cease. After the Crusades it assumed more violent forms as Papal exploitation grew, until a complete breach with the Papal Stool was effected in various countries.

The lower clergy in particular assumed the leadership in the struggle with Rome; the Reformers were priests— Luther, Zwingli, Calvin, etc.; and the lesser clergy marked out the intellectual lines which the Reformation struggles were to follow.

But while the Church of the early Middle Ages was the force that held the State and society together, at the time of the Reformation the Church was a mere tool of the political administration; the basis of the State had changed. When the national Church broke away from Rome, it parted with the traditional illusions that alone could have perpetuated its rule in the State. Consequently the clergy of the Reformed Churches became servants of the State power, or officials of absolutism. The Church no longer determined what men should believe and how they should act; the State power prescribed what the Church should teach.

Not all nations and not all classes in the nations had an interest in separation from the Papacy. Nobody in Italy for instance.

The ruler of the Hapsburg countries, the Emperor, also had no interest in the Reformation. His power in Germany was as unsubstantial as that of the Popes; it was partly based on illusions doomed to disappear. To expect the Emperor to cut adrift from the Pope was to expect him to commit suicide.

Nor was he interested in the Reformation as ruler of the variegated Hapsburg lands, in the cohesion of which Catholicism was a potent element.

Only under his leadership could a Crusade of the whole of Christendom against the Turks be undertaken, which would primarily have strengthened the House of Hapsburg. With the Reformation every hope of such a Crusade vanished.

Just as little cause had the rulers of France and Spain to separate from Rome. In these countries the kingly power was at that time preponderant. In both countries trade and commodity production had developed at an early

period, earliest of all in Southern France, where the first
revolt against the Papal power had broken out, the
" heresy " of the Albigenses, who were exterminated in
a bloody war at the beginning of the thirteenth century.
But where the city republics of Southern France had
failed, the kings of France at a later date succeeded.
In 1269 Saint Louis issued a pragmatic sanction, which
was renewed and extended by Charles VI. in 1438. This
made the French clergy to a large extent independent
of Rome and placed them under the king, thus practically
achieving what the German princes accomplished during
the Reformation nearly a hundred years later. The
king made the higher clerical appointments and it was
forbidden to raise money for the Pope without the king's
consent.

Similarly in Spain. From 1480 onwards the Inquisition
itself became the police force of the kingly power, which
appointed the inquisitors and made the institution subservient to its political ends. From Spain no more than
from France could the Pope obtain money without the
royal permission.

The permission to sell indulgences, which gave the
impulse to the Reformation, was dearly bought by Leo X.
in France and Spain. Charles V. received a loan of 175,000
ducats; Francis I. of France took a nice share of the proceeds of the indulgences. Of the German princes only the
Elector of Mainz was strong enough as a spiritual and
secular priest to obtain a share of the spoil. The other
German princes received nothing, which aroused their
indignation and inclined them towards the Reformation.

Not only had the kings and the clergy of France and
Spain, in consequence of the higher economic development
of their countries, practically obtained before the Reformation what the princes and clergy in Germany had to wrest
in a severe struggle, but they had become strong enough

to try and make the Pope himself their tool and exploit his influence and power for themselves. Thus it was in their interest to maintain his rule over Christendom, which was in truth their rule.

At the beginning of the fourteenth century the French kings had become strong enough to compel the submission of the Popes of Rome, who established themselves on French soil, at Avignon, from 1308 to 1377. It was not the influence of the Church, but the strengthening of Italy and of the national and monarchical idea itself, concomitant with the economic development, which enabled the Pope finally to break away from France and withdraw to Rome. But now the French began their attempts to subjugate Italy, including the Pope. The same attempt was made by Spain, whose position was most favourable at the beginning of the Reformation, when Charles united the German Imperial Crown with the Spanish Crown.

Just when the German princes were cautiously and tentatively trying to escape from the yoke of the Papacy, the two great Catholic powers were locked in fierce combat for its control.

In the year 1521 Pope Leo X. submitted to the Emperor Charles V., and in the same year the latter placed Luther under the ban of the Empire. Hadrian VI., Leo's successor, was "a creature of his Imperial Majesty," and when Clement VII., who followed Hadrian, endeavoured to become independent of the Emperor, this defender of the Catholic faith sent his mercenary army against the "Holy Father," stormed Rome, and devastated the city.

That Italy, France, and Spain remained Catholic is not to be ascribed to their spiritual backwardness, but rather to their higher economic development. They were the masters of the Pope; through him they exploited Teutonic Christendom, which was compelled to separate from the

Papacy in order to escape exploitation, but at the cost of severing its ties with the wealthiest and most highly developed countries in Europe. In so far the Reformation was a struggle of barbarism against civilisation.

It was not by chance that the brunt of the Reformation fell on two of the most backward nations of Europe: Sweden and Scotland.

This is, of course, not to be understood as a condemnation of the Reformation. We have recorded the above facts because it explains why the most cultivated minds in Germany as in England would have nothing to do with the Reformation, a phenomenon which is unintelligible if we adopt the traditional view that the Reformation was essentially of a spiritual nature, a struggle between Protestant light and Catholic darkness.

On the contrary, Humanism was in complete antagonism to the Reformation.

CHAPTER IV

HUMANISM

1. *Paganism and Catholicism.*

THE new method of production also fostered new modes of thinking and created a new content of thought. The content of mental life changed quicker than its forms; the latter long remained the ecclesiastical forms corresponding to the feudal mode of production, while ideas were more and more influenced by commodity production and assumed a secular character.

Nevertheless the traditional ecclesiastical forms could not long suffice for the new modes of thought, which could dispense with these forms the more easily as ready to hand for immediate use was a form of thought which had formerly served to express an intellectual content coincident in many respects with the new mode of thought. This form of thought was the science and art of Antiquity.

Commodity production, which supplanted the feudal mode of production, first developed in Italy, the country in which antique paganism had left many brilliant vestiges, and where its traditions had never quite died out. The thriving commercial traffic with Greece also made the Italians acquainted with the ancient Hellenic literature, which accorded better with the new mode of thought than the Roman. The Italian commercial republics, which strove to free themselves from the constraints of feudalism, both mental and material, were enchanted to find in the literature of the old commercial republic of Athens a mode of thought which resembled in so many points their own, just as the material life in both places revealed great similarities—a mode of thought which had developed to its most brilliant expression. What an infant mode of production would otherwise have had laboriously to create, a new philosophy, a new science and art, had only to be disinterred by the intellectual representatives of the new mode of production from the ruins of Antiquity.

The study of Antiquity began with the object of understanding the present and dealing a death-blow to the expiring vestiges of the most recent past. The intellectual tendency which developed under the influence of this study is known as the Renaissance (rebirth, notably of Antiquity) and as Humanism (the striving after a purely human culture, in contrast to scholastic theology, which is concerned with divine things). The former title indicates the expression of the new tendency in art, the latter in literature.

If ideas really created material conditions, and not the reverse, a resurrection of antique society ought to have proceeded from the revival of antique ideas. No mode of thinking has perhaps been adopted with such enthusiasm as were the antique ideas by the Humanists. Yet they only adopted these ideas in the degree that they corresponded with actual conditions.

In Antiquity as in the Middle Ages commodity production and commerce arose in the city republics. But what had been in Antiquity the zenith of social development was at the close of the Middle Ages the starting-point of a new society.

We have already seen how the beginnings of the capitalist mode of production fostered the growth of absolute monarchy and nationalism. Thus the Humanists became the most zealous champions of national unity under one prince, despite their enthusiasm for Demosthenes and Cicero, and despite the fact that many of them came from city republics.

The father of Humanism, the Florentine Dante (1265-1321), declared himself a monarchist and a glowing enthusiast for the unity of Italy, to accomplish which he had to appeal to the German Emperor, as the Popes of his time were tools of France. But after the return of the Popes from Avignon, they become the power around which the majority of the Italian Humanists gathered and from which they expected the unity of Italy.

Most Humanists held the view that the developing modern State required a head. But just because, in their opinion, the weal and woe of the State depended on the personality of the prince—and this opinion was in their time justified by the conditions—it was assuredly not a matter of indifference what kind of prince it was. Just as necessary as the rule of a prince in the State, just as necessary, in the opinion of the Humanists, was it that they themselves ruled the princes, that they educated and guided the princes. How far the implications of this standpoint were realised depended on the personal character of the individual. A prince was, of course, necessary for the welfare of the people, but only a good prince—that is, a prince educated on Humanist lines. To offer resistance to a bad prince, to depose, even to murder him, in order to make room for a better prince, in no way contradicted the principles of Humanism, although few Humanists mustered sufficient courage to give practical effect to their teachings. Many of them were supine flatterers. But usually they asserted their claim to rule the princes intellectually. This is confirmed by the numerous Humanist publications designed to give counsel to princes as to how they should organise and govern their States, the best known work of this class being Macchiavelli's *The Prince*.

Moreover, it was no empty claim that the Humanists made. They were in fact a power which the princes needed and were disposed to accept. The princes required not merely the material resources of the bourgeoisie, but also the services of its ideologists. " Public opinion "—that is, the ideas of the urban burgher population—was a force, and in the times and countries where Humanism flourished it was dominated by Humanism. The princes needed the scholars of the new movement for the business of government. No bureaucracy had yet been formed. Apart from the lawyers and the higher clergy, the only persons able to conduct administration and to act as counsellors and ambassadors of princes were to be found among the Humanists.

With the exception of certain German provinces, where the rulers practically ignored the Humanists, every prince sought to attract to his Court as many Humanists as possible, and almost princely honours were bestowed on an eminent scholar. Scholars were then the chosen friends of princes. It is partly to this circumstance that Henry VIII.'s behaviour to More is to be ascribed.

The Humanists were no more logical in their religious views than in their political. While, on the one hand, they combined enthusiasm for the antique republicans with devotion to the monarchy, on the other hand, they were largely Pagan in their outlook and yet remained staunch Catholics withal. As the new mode of production was opposed to the feudal mode, so the new outlook contrasted with the feudal outlook. The more the old mode of production decayed, the more boldly the Humanists thrust all traditional obstacles aside, mocking the family and marriage forms of the Middle Ages as much as its religion.

The emancipation of woman signifies her partial freedom from household duties, which is possible only if the heavy household labours become public services. It could, however, also be achieved if the housewife were able to shift the work of the household on to others. This would emancipate one section of women at the expense of others.

The first kind of emancipation is essentially a matter for the future. The second kind has been realised ever since the ruling class has intensified its exploitation of the working class to the point of releasing both men and women of the upper class from the necessity of labour.

An example of women's emancipation through exploitation is afforded by the Roman Imperial age, and to the same category belong the modern emancipation of the middle-class woman and also the female emancipation of Humanism.

The individual household, and also a certain degree of monogamy, were economic necessities for the artisan and peasant. It was almost impossible to conduct farming or handicraft enterprise that was not connected with a well-ordered household, the latter needing a supreme mistress as much as the industrial concern a supreme master.

A peasant could keep neither labourers nor maids, a master no apprentices, without a household, without a housewife; for apprentices and labourers belonged to the family, ate at the same table with the head, and lived in his house.

The merchant made different arrangements. As his business was independent of a household, it was of little importance whether he had a housewife or not. Marriage and a household became a luxury for him, whereas it had been an economic necessity. If he were frugal, he need not marry at all, unless he took a wife not as a house-keeper, but as an heiress. If his trading profits were large enough, he could transfer the management of his house-hold to hirelings.

Thus, in consequence of the unlimited profits of trade, the wives of merchants, and to some extent of professional men, were freed from household duties, as well as from work generally, in the course of the fifteenth and sixteenth centuries. They found time to interest themselves in questions outside their former mental horizon. But concomitant with this emancipation, the traditional form of marriage tended to become an article of luxury in mercantile and Humanist circles, resulting in a loosening of sexual ties, above all in Italy, the home of Humanism. With the impetuosity of youth the upper middle class burst the bonds of the patriarchal family, of monogamy, but just as in Imperial Rome the emancipation of woman changed her from a necessary worker into a superfluous exploiter, so something of the licentiousness of a decadent class was mingled in the new sexual standards.

Such were the elements which imparted its peculiar character to the female emancipation of Humanism. Moreover, it was restricted to a smaller social circle than modern woman's emancipation.

Just as modern champions of woman's emancipation seek to justify this change on physiological and legal grounds as something enjoined by nature and justice, and not as a special phase of history, so the Humanists at first appealed to religion, although traditional ecclesiastical doctrine was emphatically opposed to the equality of the sexes.

The boldness of Humanism in the sphere of sex was carried into the religious sphere. At the outset Pagan scepticism still wore an ecclesiastical vestment, but it became more and more open in the course of time, and would have led to complete atheism (of the Humanists, not of the masses), had not the development been checked by the Reformation.

2. *Paganism and Protestantism.*

Ecclesiastical abuses were vigorously attacked by all Humanists, and monkery in particular was the chosen target of their ridicule.

But however sharp these attacks were they stopped at a certain point. The logic of facts imposed illogical thought on the Humanists.

We have seen in the preceding chapter that the ruling and exploiting classes of the Romance countries, especially of Italy, had a great interest in maintaining the power of the Papacy. The ideologists of the new social forces in the Romance countries were obliged to give expression to this Papal sentiment, whether it fitted into their system or not. As a fact, nearly all the Humanists—the more important without exception—attacked not the institutions of the Church, but the persons of its members and the spirit which animated them. The existing forms of the Church should be retained, but new wine should be poured into the old bottles. While remaining a comprehensive and omnipotent institution, the Church should become a Humanist Church, the Humanists being her priests (and holders of her fat benefices), and the Pope the supreme Humanist. As such, he should rule princes and peoples through the agency of Humanists, and promote Humanist objects.

An illustration of this is the Rabelaisian ideal monastery of the Thelemites. In chapters 52 to 57 of *Gargantua*, Rabelais describes the imaginary abbey of Thelema, which is run quite on Humanist lines. In our view the description of the monastery is informed by just as serious a purpose as More's *Utopia*. It shows us the way in which Humanism would reform the Church. The exploitation of the masses by the Church would continue —even the abbey of Thelema is inconceivable apart from exploitation—but Humanists will take the place of the monks, and freedom of enjoyment and science will reign instead of ascetic rules of conduct.

The peculiar position of Italy, from whose soil Humanism germinated, impelled Humanism to adopt a friendly attitude towards the Papacy, which was not only in contradiction to its theoretical basis, but also to the needs of the social forces outside the Romance countries, to which it purported to give expression. Humanism went to pieces on this rock once the superior position of Italy vanished.

In Italy Humanism responded to real interests, but this was not the case in the Teutonic countries, where it remained an exotic plant which could strike no roots in the soil. German Humanism had therefore every reason for close union with Italy, whence came all science and art. Only by continuing this connection could the Humanists hope to get the better of the Northern barbarism and win the support of the powerful classes. Separation from Rome signified the shattering of their hopes, and the victory of barbarism over civilisation. Consequently, they opposed the Reformation and remained Catholic precisely because they stood at a higher level of development than the Protestants, who were the bitter opponents of the new science and art.

This was not only the case with the Northern Reformers; the Reformation movement in Italy also proceeded from the semi-peasant lower clergy. Take, for example, Savonarola. In one of his sermons he said: "The sole good that Plato and Aristotle have accomplished is that they have adduced many arguments that can be turned against heretics.   Yet they and other philosophers remain in hell.   An old woman knows more of faith than Plato. It would be a good thing for faith if many books otherwise apparently useful were destroyed.   If there were not so many books and not so many disputes, faith would grow more quickly than it has hitherto done.''   Who does not remember Luther's outburst against the "Whore Reason"!   The pious Savonarola caused hundreds of copies of Boccaccio's *Decameron* to be burnt, until the Church put an end to his activity and executed him as a heretic.

Papal exploitation was threatened, not by the sceptics who spoke to the educated, but by the pious-minded who addressed the masses.   Sceptics, like Rabelais, who poured the most scornful mockery on the Church and the faith, were spared by bishops and Popes, and not infrequently encouraged.   The Catholic fanaticism of the Papacy was not a fanaticism of faith, but a fanaticism of avarice clothed in ecclesiastical forms.

When fighting on the Catholic side, in order to defend the threatened civilisation, the learned ideologists of Germany and England forgot, however, one thing: that this Catholic culture, the high status of science and art in Italy, the grandeur of the Papacy, were based on the ignorance and exploitation of the masses, the ignorance and exploitation of the whole of Germany; that the Papacy was obliged to keep Germany poor and illiterate in order to promote science and art in Italy; that it was a barbarism artificially maintained by the Popes themselves which overthrew Catholic culture during the Reformation; that the historical situation was of such a nature that only the victory of German barbarism over Romance civilisation could liberate Germany from barbarism and make possible her further economic and mental development.

The Humanists were alive only to the injury to science

and art which the Reformation would inflict, at least temporarily, in the Northern countries. They had another reason for adhesion to Catholicism. The Reformers appealed to the masses, to the whole people. In the various countries of the Reformation the entire people confronted the Papacy as a single class, the exploited class. With the exception of England, where the Reformation assumed a peculiar character, the Reformation countries were economically backward lands, where absolutism had not developed to the point it had reached in the Romance countries, where peasants and knights still possessed a certain degree of power. If the princes and the money powers eventually derived the greatest advantage from the Reformation, it is none the less true that the latter began as a popular movement, as a brave revolt of the whole people against Papal exploitation, a revolt which did not stop with the overthrow of Papal rule, but led to fierce struggles between the various classes, draining their strength and preparing the way for the victory of princely absolutism.

The Humanists detested popular movements. Any government except by a prince, any influence over the State save that exerted through the person of a prince, seemed to them utterly perverse. Usually they had little sympathy with or interest in the needs and aspirations of the people. They regarded with horror a movement which unchained all the abominations of civil war.

Under these circumstances, it is easy to understand that in most Teutonic countries their partisanship for Catholicism set them in antagonism to the whole people; that they were branded as renegades by the Reformers, and finally disappeared without leaving a trace of their influence on the people.

The Reformation also sounded the death-knell of Humanism in Italy. The sea route to India round the

Cape of Good Hope was already discovered, and the new trade routes which connected India with Europe until the opening of the Suez Canal were already being used. Commerce passed from the coastwise Mediterranean countries to the countries on the Atlantic seaboard. Simultaneously the Teutonic countries broke out in rebellion against the Papacy, and the huge sums of money which year by year had flowed over the Alps to Rome were no longer forthcoming. The sources of Italy's wealth dried up and her intellectual greatness suffered eclipse. Trade and exploitation had been the material basis of Humanism, and as they dwindled, so Humanism disappeared. But not entirely. Its tendencies were revived in Jesuitism. Jesuitism is Humanism at a lower mental level, robbed of its spiritual independence, rigidly organised and pressed in the service of the Church. Jesuitism resembles Humanism as the Christianity of the Imperial age resembled Neoplatonism. It is the form in which the Catholic Church embraced Humanism and brought herself up to date, abandoning the feudal outlook for the outlook which dominated society from the sixteenth to the eighteenth centuries. Jesuitism became the most formidable power of the reformed Catholic Church because it was more in harmony with the new economic and political conditions. It wrought its effects by virtue of the same forces that Humanism had made use of: by the superiority of classical education, by influencing princes and paying heed to the financial powers. Like the Humanists, the Jesuits fostered absolute power, but only in the case of the princes for whom they laboured. Like the Humanists, they did not think it incompatible with their monarchical sentiments to remove princes who did not suit their purposes.

With regard to money, however, the Jesuits went

further than the Humanists. They became the greatest trading company of Europe, with branches in all parts of the world. They were the first to perceive how the missionary could be utilised as a commercial traveller; they were the first to establish capitalist undertakings, such as sugar factories, overseas.

3. *Scepticism and Superstition.*

Humanism led logically to a complete denial of the medieval philosophy, to pure scepticism. But instead of this, there appeared at the close of its career, as its heir, a fiercer religious fanaticism than the Middle Ages ever knew, and this in its own native land, in Italy, as well as in the countries where it had never gained a footing.

This is to be ascribed not alone to the economic eclipse of Italy, and the embitterment of the struggle between the exploiting Italians and the exploited nations, which transmuted the fanaticism of avarice into the fanaticism of faith, faith being the title by virtue of which this exploitation was carried on. The strengthening of religious life towards the close of the epoch of Humanism was grounded more and more in the contemporary conditions.   One of the roots of religion in the age of Humanism was somewhat perished, but from the second root there sprouted luxurious shoots.

The intellectual roots of religion, the causes of religious thought and feeling lie in the existence of superhuman and incomprehensible forces, in face of which man is helpless, whose operations he can neither control nor foresee, and which exert such a decisive influence upon his weal and woe that he feels the need of propitiating them.

These forces are either natural or social forces.

Under primitive communism the social forces play no part. There the fate of mankind is settled by economic conditions, so far as they depend upon social co-operation. At this primitive stage man is all the more dependent upon nature. He still feels himself to be part of nature, like an animal, he has not yet broken away from nature's umbilical cord, and so dreams his days away. Of religion there is as yet little mention.

Slowly, as a concomitant of technical progress, there arises in man the need to subdue Nature to his will; he breaks away from her, and she becomes an object distinct from him, to investigate which is his task. But man's first experience as he travels this path is a sense of impotence in face of nature; an enormous epoch must pass away, a long historic development must work itself out, before man begins to understand Nature, perceive her laws, and make deliberate use of her forces.

Religion becomes a human need from the moment man begins to ponder upon nature until the rise of the natural sciences.

The religions created by this need, the nature religions, are serene, joyous, and tolerant, like the men in whose minds they grew; natural phenomena are bountiful and divine rather than awe-inspiring and devilish.

The rise of commodity production brought into existence social forces which man cannot control, and thus the second root of religion germinated. In the small communities of Antiquity and the Middle Ages this second root remains quiescent. The economic conditions may there be more easily surveyed, and luck and mishap appear usually as the result of personal conduct, explicable without calling in a superhuman force. Social phenomena must become mass phenomena before men become aware of the social forces and realise their impotence in face of them, before the social forces can captivate the imagination and the reason and exercise a decisive influence on the character of religion.

The nature religions are essentially local; the social religions that supplanted them are from the start mass religions, world religions.

For such a religion the Roman world-empire prepared the soil. The social phenomena then existing were eminently favourable to its rise. Mass poverty and mass disease side by side with the pride and avarice of a few excessively rich persons, the depopulation and decadence of the whole Empire—under these auspices Christianity came into being. Anxiety and despair, enmity and sanguinary lust seized hold of men. The serene deities of Paganism were transformed into horrid demons, the Creator and Judge of the world became sinister and relentless, the slightest fault was punished with everlasting torture, the whole world became a forecourt of hell, filled with devils greedily seeking whom they might devour.

Into this burst the primitive Teutons, who inspired Christianity with their joyous spirit. Their gods were indeed changed into demons and devils, but the devil lost his terrors. The devil of the Middle Ages was a good-humoured, harmless devil, with whom one condescended to play, and whom one mocked with impunity. The Crucified One with the crown of thorns receded into the background, and the benevolent Saviour, the Good Shepherd, became the favourite figure of the Church, and after him the Blessed Virgin, a feminine ideal, invested with all the tenderness which Germans revere in their women.

The elaboration of ecclesiastical dogmas received a check in these " dark ages," but the Church festivals were the more zealously observed.

It is a remarkable fact that as Humanism evolved towards freethought, the popular religion tended to lose its earlier character and reverted to the Christianity of the Imperial age. This is only explicable in the light of the economic transformation that was then proceeding.

It is true that commodity production and commerce promoted the natural sciences, and these two factors reciprocally influenced each other. Intercourse with the East brought to the West not only the commodities, but also the learning of antique civilisations. But this had very little influence on religion at the time.

Humanism developed primarily under the stimulation of the classical, antique literature, from which natural science had little to glean. Very few scholars educated on Humanist lines devoted their attention to the departments of science in which the Arabs had done pioneer work—anatomy, chemistry, and astronomy—in order to investigate the laws of nature methodically, and thus prepare the great scientific discoveries of the sixteenth and seventeenth centuries. Most of those who devoted themselves to the natural sciences did so with an eye to the immediate use they could make of such studies. And where the transmitted knowledge was inadequate, it was eked out by speculations and hypotheses, supported by quotations from the old writers.

Men did not turn to the study of the human and animal body and its functions, but strove to acquire magic formulas for curing disease. Anatomy made slow progress, but quackery spread with lightning rapidity. The herding of the people in large towns, exhibiting the extremes of riches and poverty, prepared the soil for epidemics and diseases.

As with medicine, so with chemistry. It had mastered the art of resolving bodies into their elements and reconstituting them out of their elements. What easier than to exploit it for the manufacture of that metal after which everyone panted—gold ? Chemistry was degraded into alchemy.

Astronomical knowledge spread rapidly among the scholars in the age of Humanism and of the Reformation.

In navigation it could be applied to practical purposes. Without it, overseas commerce would have been impossible, and so it was cultivated with zeal. The laws of astronomy, taken over from the ancients, were almost the only natural laws then known at all widely; but they too were soon enlisted in the service of exploitation and superstition. As the orbits of the planets could be calculated and men suspected that they influenced the earth, endeavours were made to predict earthly fates from their positions. The more uncertain their futures, the greedier men were to explore them. The stars became their consolation in that revolutionary time when the firmament seemed the only fixed point. But it, too, was eventually revolutionised.

Astrology, alchemy, and quackery were the forms in which the natural sciences in Europe were first known to the masses, and even to the majority of educated people at the close of the Middle Ages. This kind of " natural science " was not calculated to undermine the need for religion.

The scepticism of the Humanists, in fact, was merely the outcome of the absurdity of existing beliefs or of indifference; it did not arise from a scientific insight into the processes of nature.

While the natural sciences failed to kill one of the roots of religion, its other root received a powerful stimulus from the economic development.

The economic props of the lower classes were vanishing, chief among them being the village communities which had carried the people through the storms of the Middle Ages. New class struggles broke out, of a more fearful kind than those of feudal times. The latter were mostly concerned with increasing or reducing rights and duties, but now the nascent and the declining classes were locked in life-and-death grapples. The oppression and impoverishment of the peasants, misery and vagabondage, increased. Attempts to put down the mishandled classes assumed an increasingly brutal and bloody character, the convulsive efforts of the tortured peoples to shake off the yoke of bondage became ever more violent. Hatred, anxiety, and despair were permanent guests in the cottage and in the palace. Everybody trembled at the future, lamented the past, and grappled with the present. War became a vocation, slaughter a handicraft. The discharged soldier was compelled by necessity to continue the usages of war in time of peace, and those he threatened were driven to hunt him like a wild beast. And simultaneously plague and syphilis raged through Europe. Everywhere was insecurity, misery, constant anxiety in face of the irresistible social forces, forces which did not operate within the narrow limits of the village community, but swept through mankind with the devastating breath of an international scourge.

This situation powerfully stimulated the religious need, the longing for a better hereafter, the impulse to recognise an omnipotent God, who alone seemed able to make an end of the universal misery. At the same time religion lost its serene and benevolent character, and developed its darker and crueller sides. The devil reappeared, and men's imaginations were busy painting him in the blackest colours. The torments of hell were revived and partially realised on earth in the cruelties inflicted upon the living. Witch hunting and witch burning were concomitants of the bloody legislation against beggars and vagabonds.

This transformation was long preparing in the minds of the masses, and it was the Reformation that first brought it to light. That movement not only shattered the tradition of the old popular religion; it also fired all the class antagonisms which had hitherto been simmering beneath the surface of society, and thereby released the tendencies of the age of the primitive accumulation of capital which have been described above. Superstition and fanaticism, cruelty and bloodthirstiness, developed to insane lengths. From the Peasant War to the Peace of Westphalia (1525 to 1648) Europe resembled a madhouse.

During this century, what we know to-day as religion was evolved—the various Protestant sects and Jesuitical, Tridentine Catholicism. The old Catholicism of feudal times, as practised by the people and not by the Papal Court, has disappeared, and only in a remote mountain village is there to be found some faint traces of the joviality and joyousness of Teutonic Christianity.

The leaders of the Enlightenment movement of the eighteenth century found in the new religion their most dangerous enemy, and the greatest obstacle interposed between them and the people on the one hand and the monarchy on the other hand. In its contest with this religion the Enlightenment movement became great. Historians who followed in the paths marked out by the Enlightenment philosophy described all religions and the Christianity of all ages in terms of the religion with which the Enlightenment movement grappled. They misunderstood the Teutonic-Catholic popular religion of the Middle Ages all the more readily as the character of early Christianity exhibited a striking similarity with the Christianity of the Reformation period, and only scanty material was available concerning the popular religion of the Middle Ages which was intermediate between the two.

To persist in this error, however, would lead to an entirely wrong estimate of the Middle Ages. In particular—and this is the reason for our discussion—it would lead to a wholly one-sided conception of Thomas More. To Voltaire, for instance, More seemed a narrow-minded, fanatical barbarian on account of his obstinate adherence to Catholicism.

More died as a martyr to Catholicism. To understand him we must know what kind of Catholicism he adhered to. We must therefore keep constantly in mind the difference between the old, feudal, popular Catholicism and the modern Jesuitical Catholicism. More was one of the last representatives of the former, so far as he was a Catholic at all, neither a hypocrite nor an intriguer, but a man in the best sense of the word.

Having described the general historical situation in which More grew up, we will turn to the circumstances of his career.

PART II
THOMAS MORE

CHAPTER I

THOMAS MORE'S BIOGRAPHERS

1. *Roper and Others.*

To most of the biographies of More a certain fragrance of incense clings, which is not the incense which a grateful posterity burns to men who have done gallant service for mankind, but the incense which the Catholic Church burns to its saints in order to intoxicate the senses of the faithful.

More, in fact, died a Catholic martyr, and the Catholic Church has not produced so many eminent thinkers and outstanding personalities since the Reformation that it could become tired of extolling the fame of More to its own greater glory. Not everything that More did or wrote was glorious in the sight of the Catholic Church, and for this reason the biographies of More are somewhat one-sided.

The most unprejudiced is the earliest of his biographies, written by his son-in-law, William Roper, probably in the year 1557.

Roper lived in More's house for sixteen years; he is an honest fellow, simple and sober, and we may place full reliance on his narrative. But Roper was too small a man to realise the significance of More's intellectual contribution to his age. Roper does not mention that More wrote *Utopia*.

Of greater mental calibre was the next of More's biographers, Thomas Stapleton, an English Catholic priest, who wrote a biography of More while living in exile at Douai. His book was published in 1588. He supplements Roper by the details he furnishes of More's literary activity. His book, however, is not a historical study, but a work of edification, a hotch-potch of anecdotes, legends, and miraculous stories.

A biography of More by his great-grandson, Cresacre More, appeared in 1627, a second edition of which was issued one hundred years later. This work has not the slightest value, apart from some convenient extracts from Roper and Stapleton which it contains.

The great majority of the subsequent Catholic biographies of More are more or less bad paraphrases of Cresacre More's book.

Nor has Protestant literature produced any important biography of More. Cayley's book is mediocre so far as it is biography, but valuable for its account of More's best literary achievements.

Apart from the three original sources above mentioned, only four biographies need be referred to: the Catholics Rudhart and Bridgett and the Protestants Seebohm and Hutten. Seebohm discussed an aspect of More that had hitherto received little attention: More as a Humanist in his relations with the two other Humanists then in England, Colet and Erasmus. T. C. Bridgett, a Catholic priest, wrote his book in glorification of the Catholic Martyr who was pronounced a saint in 1886.

Hutten likewise composed his work with a theological bias, and endeavoured to show that More's theology was compatible with the Church of England.

In view of such biographies, the student who desires to understand More the Socialist will turn with relief to More's own writings and a great part of his letters, in which he reveals his whole mind. More's writings composed in English were published in London in 1557, by command of Queen Mary.

2. *Erasmus of Rotterdam.*

The best contemporary description of More's career and character is contained in a letter which Erasmus of Rotterdam addressed to Ulrich von Hutten, which we transcribe almost entire:

" Most illustrious Hutten—Your love, I had almost said your passion for the genius of Thomas More—kindled as it is by his writings, which, as you truly say, are as learned and witty as anything can possibly be—is, I assure you, shared by many others; and moreover the feeling in this case is mutual; since More is so delighted with what you have written, that I am myself almost jealous of you. It is an example of what Plato says of that sweetest wisdom, which excites much more ardent love among men than the most admirable beauty of form. It is not discerned by the eye of sense, but the mind has eyes of its own, so that even here the Greek saying holds true, that out of looking grows liking, and so it comes to pass that people are sometimes united in the warmest affection, who have never seen or spoken to each other. And, as it is a common experience, that for some unexplained reason different people are attracted by different kinds of beauty, so between one mind and another, there seems to be a sort of latent kindred, which causes us to be specially delighted with some minds and not with others.

" As to your asking me to paint you a full-length portrait of More, I only wish my power of satisfying your request were equal to your earnestness in pressing it. For to me, too, it will be no unpleasant task to linger awhile in the contemplation of a friend, who is the most delightful character in the world. But, in the first place, it is not given to every man to be aware of all More's accomplishments; and in the next place, I know not whether he will himself like to have his portrait painted by any artist that chooses to do so. For indeed I do not think it more easy to make a likeness of More than of Alexander the Great or of Achilles; neither were those heroes more worthy of immortality. The hand of an Apelles is required for such a subject, and I am afraid I am more like a Fulvius or a Rutuba than an Apelles. Nevertheless I will try to draw you a sketch, rather than a portrait of the entire man, so far as daily and domestic intercourse has enabled me to observe his likeness and retain it in my memory. But if some diplomatic employment should ever bring you together, you will find out, how poor an artist you have chosen for this commission; and I am afraid you will think me guilty of envy or of wilful blindness in taking note of so few out of the many good points of his character.

" To begin with that part of him which is least known to you—in shape and stature More is not a tall man, but not remarkably short, all his limbs being so symmetrical, that no deficiency is observed in this respect. His complexion is fair, being rather blonde than pale, but with no approach to redness, except a very delicate flush, which lights up the whole. His hair is auburn inclining to black, or if you like it better, black inclining to auburn; his beard thin, his eyes a bluish grey with some sort of tinting upon them. This kind of eye is thought to be a sign of the happiest character, and is regarded with favour in England, whereas with us black eyes are rather preferred. It is said, that no kind of eye is so free from defects of sight.

His countenance answers for his character, having an expression of kind and friendly cheerfulness with a little air of raillery. To speak candidly, it is a face more expressive of pleasantry than of gravity or dignity, though very far removed from folly or buffoonery. His right shoulder seems a little higher than his left, especially when he is walking, a peculiarity that is not innate, but the result of habit, like many tricks of the kind. In the rest of his body there is nothing displeasing, only his hands are a little coarse, or appear so, as compared with the rest of his figure. He has always from his boyhood been very negligent of his toilet, so as not to give much attention even to the things which according to Ovid are all that men need care about. What a charm there was in his looks when young, may even now be inferred from what remains; although I knew him myself when he was not more than three-and-twenty years old; for he has not yet passed much beyond his fortieth year. His health is sound rather than robust, but sufficient for any labours suitable to an honourable citizen; and we may fairly hope that his life may be long, as he has a father living of a great age, but an age full of freshness and vigour.

"I have never seen any person less fastidious in his choice of food. As a young man, he was by preference a water-drinker, a practice he derived from his father. But, not to give annoyance to others, he used at table to conceal this habit from his guests by drinking, out of a pewter vessel, either small beer almost as weak as water, or plain water. As to wine, it being the custom where he was for the company to invite each other to drink in turn of the same cup, he used sometimes to sip a little of it, to avoid appearing to shrink from it altogether, and to habituate himself to the common practice. For his eating he has been accustomed to prefer beef and salt meats, and household bread thoroughly fermented to those articles of diet which are commonly regarded as delicacies. But he does not shrink from things that impart an innocent pleasure, even of a bodily kind, and has always a good appetite for milk puddings and for fruit, and eats a dish of eggs with the greatest relish.

" His voice is neither loud nor excessively low, but of a penetrating tone. It has nothing in it melodious or soft, but is simply suitable for speech, as it does not seem to have any natural talent for singing, though he takes pleasure in music of every kind. His articulation is wonderfully distinct, being equally free from hurry and from hesitation.

" He likes to be dressed simply, and does not wear silk, or purple, or gold chains, except when it is not allowable to dispense with them. He cares marvellously little for those formalities which with ordinary people are the test of politeness, and as he does not exact these ceremonies from others, so he is not scrupulous in observing them himself, either on occasions of meeting or at entertainments, though he understands how to use them, if he thinks proper to do so; but he holds it to be effeminate and unworthy of a man to waste much of his time on such trifles.

" He was formerly rather disinclined to a Court life and to any intimacy with princes, having always a special hatred of tyranny and a great fancy for equality; whereas you will scarcely find any Court so well-ordered, as not to have much bustle and ambition and pretence and luxury, or to be free from tyranny in some form or other. He could not even be tempted to Henry the Eighth's Court without great trouble although nothing could be desired more courteous or less exacting than this prince. He is naturally fond of liberty and leisure; but as he enjoys a holiday when he has it, so whenever business requires it no one is more vigilant or more patient.

" He seems to be born and made for friendship, of which

he is the sincerest and most persistent devotee. Neither is he afraid of that multiplicity of friends, of which Hesiod disapproves. Accessible to every tender of intimacy, he is by no means fastidious in choosing his acquaintance, while he is most accommodating in keeping it on foot, and constant in retaining it. If he has fallen in with anyone whose faults he cannot cure, he finds some opportunity of parting with him, untying the knot of intimacy without tearing it; but when he has found any sincere friends, whose characters are suited to his own, he is so delighted with their society and conversation, that he seems to find in these the chief pleasure of life, having an absolute distaste for tennis and dice and cards, and the other games with which the mass of gentlemen beguile the tediousness of Time. It should be added that, while he is somewhat neglectful of his own interest, no one takes more pains in attending to the concerns of his friends. What more need I say? If anyone requires a perfect example of his true friendship, it is in More that he will best find it.

" In company his extraordinary kindness and sweetness of temper are such as to cheer the dullest spirit, and alleviate the annoyance of the most trying circumstances. From boyhood he was always so pleased with a joke, that it might seem that jesting was the main object of his life; but with all that, he did not go so far as buffoonery, nor had ever any inclination to bitterness. When quite a youth, he wrote farces and acted them. If a thing was facetiously said, even though it was aimed at himself, he was charmed with it, so much did he enjoy any witticism that had a flavour of subtlety or genius. This led to his amusing himself as a young man with epigrams, and taking great delight in Lucian. Indeed, it was he that suggested my writing the *Moria*, or *Praise of Folly*, which was much the same thing as setting a camel to dance.

"There is nothing that occurs in human life from which

he does not seek to extract some pleasure, although the matter may be serious in itself. If he has to do with the learned and intelligent, he is delighted with their cleverness; if with unlearned or stupid people, he finds amusement in their folly. He is not offended even by professed clowns as he adapts himself with marvellous dexterity to the tastes of all; while with ladies generally and even with his wife, his conversation is made up of humour and playfulness. You would say it was a second Democritus, or rather that Pythagorean philosopher, who strolls in leisurely mood through the market-place, contemplating the turmoil of those who buy or sell. There is no one less guided by the opinion of the multitude, but on the other hand no one sticks more closely to common sense.

" One of his amusements is in observing the forms, characters and instincts of different animals. Accordingly, there is scarcely any kind of bird that he does not keep about his residence, and the same of other animals not quite so common, as monkeys, foxes, ferrets, weasels, and the like. Besides these, if he meets with any strange object, imported from abroad or otherwise remarkable, he is most eager to buy it, and has his big house so well supplied with these objects, that there is something in every room which catches your eye, as you enter it; and his own pleasure is renewed every time that he sees others interested.

" When of a sentimental age, he was not a stranger to the emotions of love, but without loss of character, having no inclination to press his advantage, and being more attracted by a mutual liking than by any licentious object.

" He had drunk deep of Good Letters from his earliest years; and when a young man he applied himself to the study of Greek and of Philosophy; but his father was so far from encouraging him in this pursuit, that he withdrew his allowance and almost disowned him, because he thought he was deserting his hereditary study, being himself an expert professor of English Law. For remote as that profession is from true learning, those who become masters of it have the highest rank and reputation among their countrymen; and it is difficult to find any readier way to acquire fortune and honour. Indeed, a considerable part of the nobility of that island has had its origin in this profession, in which it is said that no one can be perfect, unless he has toiled at it for many years. It was natural that in his younger days our friend's genius, born of better things, should shrink from this study; nevertheless, after he had had a taste of the learning of the Schools, he became so conversant with it, that there was no one more eagerly consulted by suitors; and the income that he made by it was not surpassed by any of those who did nothing else; such was the power and quickness of his intellect.

" He also expended considerable labour in perusing the volumes of the orthodox Fathers; and when scarcely more than a youth, he lectured publicly on the *De Civitate Dei* of Augustine before a numerous audience, old men and priests not being ashamed to take a lesson in divinity from a young layman, and not at all sorry to have done so. Meantime he applied his whole mind to religion, having some thought of taking orders, for which he prepared himself by watchings and fastings and prayers and such like exercises; wherein he showed much more wisdom than the generality of people, who rashly engage in so arduous a profession without testing themselves beforehand. And indeed there was no obstacle to his adopting this kind of life, except the fact, that he could not shake off his wish to marry. Accordingly he resolved to be a chaste husband rather than a licentious priest.

" When he married, he chose a very young girl, a lady

by birth with her character still unformed, having been
always kept in the country with her parents and sisters—
so that he was all the better able to fashion her according
to his own habits. Under his direction she was instructed
in learning and in every kind of music, and had almost
completely become just such a person as would have been
a delightful companion for his whole life, if an early death
had not carried her away. She had however borne him
several children, of whom three girls, Margaret, Alice, and
Cecily, and one boy, John, are still living.

" More did not however long remain single, but contrary to his friends' advice, a few months after his wife's
death he married a widow, more for the sake of the
management of his household than to please his own fancy,
as she is no great beauty, nor yet young, *nec bella admodum
nec puella*, as he sometimes says, but a sharp and watchful
housewife; with whom nevertheless he lives, on as sweet
and pleasant terms as if she were as young and lovely as
anyone could desire; and scarcely any husband obtains
from his wife by masterfulness and severity as much compliance as he does by blandishments and jests. Indeed,
what more compliance could he have, when he has induced
a woman who is already elderly, who is not naturally of a
yielding character, and whose mind is occupied with business, to learn to play the harp, the viol, the spinet and
the flute, and to give up every day a prescribed time to
practice ? With similar kindness he rules his whole
household, in which there are no tragic incidents, and no
quarrels. If anything of the kind should be likely, he
either calms it down or applies a remedy at once. And in
parting with any member of his household he has never
acted in a hostile spirit, or treated him as an enemy.
Indeed his house seems to have a sort of fatal felicity, no one
having lived in it without being advanced to higher fortune,
no inmate having ever had a stain upon his character.

"It would be difficult to find anyone living on such terms with a mother as he does with his stepmother. For his father had brought in one stepmother after another; and he has been as affectionate with each of them as with a mother. He has lately introduced a third, and More swears that he never saw anything better. His affection for his parents, children and sisters is such, that he neither wearies them with his love, nor ever fails in any kind attention.

"His character is entirely free from any touch of avarice. He has set aside out of his property what he thinks sufficient for his children, and spends the rest in a liberal fashion. When he was still dependent on his profession, he gave every client true and friendly counsel, with an eye to their advantage rather than his own, generally advising them that the cheapest thing they could do was to come to terms with their opponents. If he could not persuade them to do this, he pointed out how they might go to law at least expense; for there are some people whose character leads them to delight in litigation.

"In the City of London, where he was born, he acted for some years as judge in civil causes. This office, which is by no means burdensome—inasmuch as the Court sits only on Thursdays before dinner—is considered highly honourable; and no judge ever disposed of more suits, or conducted himself with more perfect integrity. In most cases he remitted the fees which are due from the litigants, the practice being for the plaintiff to deposit three groats before the hearing, and the defendant a like sum, and no more being allowed to be exacted. By such conduct he made himself extremely popular in the City.

"He had made up his mind to be contented with this position, which was sufficiently dignified without being

exposed to serious dangers. He has been thrust more
than once into an embassy, in the conduct of which he has
shown a great ability; and King Henry in consequence
would never rest until he dragged him into Court.
'Dragged him,' I say, and with reason; for no one was ever
more ambitious of being admitted into a Court, than he
was anxious to escape it. But as this excellent monarch
was resolved to pack his household with learned, serious,
intelligent and honest men, he especially insisted upon
having More among them—with whom he is on such terms
of intimacy that he cannot bear to let him go. If serious
affairs are in hand, no one gives wiser counsel; if it pleases
the King to relax his mind with agreeable conversation,
no man is better company. Difficult questions are often
arising, which require a grave and prudent judge; and these
questions are resolved by More in such a way, that both
sides are satisfied. And yet no one has ever induced him
to accept a present. What a blessing it would be for the
world, if magistrates like More were everywhere put in
office by sovereigns !

"Meantime there is no assumption of superiority.
In the midst of so great a pressure of business he remembers
his humble friends and from time to time he returns to his
beloved studies. Whatever authority he derives from
his rank, and whatever influence he enjoys by the favour
of a powerful sovereign, are employed in the service of the
public, or in that of his friends. It has always been part
of his character to be most obliging to everybody, and
marvellously ready with his sympathy; and this disposition
is more conspicuous than ever, now that his power of
doing good is greater. Some he relieves with money,
some he protects by his authority, some he promotes by
his recommendation, while those whom he cannot otherwise assist are benefited by his advice. No one is sent
away in distress, and you might call him the general

patron of all poor people. He counts it a great gain to himself, if he has relieved some oppressed person, made the path clear for one that was in difficulties, or brought back into favour one that was in disgrace. No man more readily confers a benefit, no man expects less in return. And successful as he is in so many ways—while success is generally accompanied by self-conceit, I have never seen any mortal being more free from this failing.

" I now propose to turn to the subject of those studies which have been the chief means of bringing More and me together.

" In his first youth his principal literary exercises were in verse. He afterwards wrestled for a long time to make his prose more smooth; practising his pen in every kind of writing in order to form that style, the character of which there is no occasion for me to recall, especially to you, who have his books always in your hands. He took the greatest pleasure in declamations, choosing some disputable subject, as involving a keener exercise of mind. Hence, while still a youth, he attempted a dialogue, in which he carried the defence of Plato's community even to the matter of wives! He wrote an answer to Lucian's *Tyrannicide*, in which argument it was his wish to have me for a rival, in order to test his own proficiency in this kind of writing.

" He published his *Utopia* for the purpose of showing what are the things that occasion mischief in commonwealths; having the English constitution especially in view, which he so thoroughly knows and understands. He had written the second book at his leisure, and afterwards, when he found it was required, added the first off-hand. Hence there is some inequality in the style.

" It would be difficult to find anyone more successful in speaking *ex tempore*, the happiest thoughts being attended by the happiest language; while a mind that catches and anticipates all that passes, and a ready memory, having everything as it were in stock, promptly supply whatever the time, or the occasion, demands. In disputations nothing can be imagined more acute, so that the most eminent theologians often find their match, when he meets them on their own ground. Hence John Colet, a man of keen and exact judgment, is wont to say in familiar conversation, that England has only one genius, whereas that island abounds in distinguished intellects.

"However averse he may be from all superstition, he is a steady adherent of true piety; having regular hours for his prayers, which are not uttered by rote, but from the heart. He talks with his friends about a future life in such a way as to make you feel that he believes what he says, and does not speak without the best hope. Such is More, even at Court; and there are still people who think that Christians are only to be found in monasteries."*

Such is Erasmus's account of the first modern Socialist.

* This admirable translation of Erasmus's letter to Hutten is by the hand of the late Mr. Nichols.

CHAPTER II

1. *More's Youth.*

IT is not our task to furnish a detailed biography of
More. We are only concerned here with More the Communist and his mental development in the spheres wherein
social life expressed itself; above all, the development
of his economic, political, and religious ideas. His outward life interests us here only so far as it bears on these.

More was born on February 7, 1478, in London, which,
if not yet the chief city of the world, was at least one of
the most important commercial centres of Europe, in
which the tendencies of the new mode of production
were sharply and clearly defined.

He came of an "honest but by no means eminent"
urban family, as the epitaph which he composed tells us.
His father, John More, was a King's Bench Judge, a sober,
strict, almost miserly man, who gave his son every cause
to reflect upon the economic conditions and to become
acquainted with the material conditions of life.

In accordance with contemporary custom, Thomas had
first of all to learn Latin, for which purpose he attended
St. Anthony's School in London, and later he was placed
by his father in the house of Archbishop (subsequently
Cardinal) Morton, an eminent statesman who had played
an important part in English politics, especially in the
Wars of the Roses, and who exercised a very favourable

95

influence on young Thomas. The grateful More says of Morton in the first book of *Utopia*: "He spoke both gracefully and weightily; he was eminently skilled in the law, had a vast understanding, and a prodigious memory; and those excellent talents with which Nature had furnished him were improved by study and experience. When I was in England the king depended much on his counsels, and the government seemed to be chiefly supported by him; for from his youth he had been all along practised in affairs; and having passed through many traverses of fortune, he had with great cost acquired a vast stock of wisdom, which is not soon lost when it is purchased so dear."

If through his father More became familiar with the material cares that were then weighing upon the world, the Archbishop of Canterbury taught him the nature of the forces that were then deciding the fate of the world, or at least usurping such right. Thus at an early age there came to him the desire to understand the present, above all its material problems, which the Humanists in the Northern countries generally lacked.

In spite of his youth, therefore, More was no longer a boy when he went up to Oxford University, probably in 1492 or 1493. There the new Humanistic studies had found a place alongside the old scholastic doctrines. Their chief representatives were Linacre, Grocyn, and Colet, and later Erasmus of Rotterdam, who came to Oxford as a teacher of Greek in 1498. More felt as much drawn towards the Humanists as they were towards him. Soon he was completely won over to Humanism.

More the elder seems to have become alarmed when his son applied himself to the unprofitable study of the classics. Somewhat unceremoniously, as Erasmus tells us, More was taken away from the University and placed in a school of English law, New Inn, probably about

1494 or 1495. Here, and later in Lincoln's Inn, Thomas studied law for several years, and afterwards acquired an extensive practice as a lawyer.

2. *More as Humanist Writer.*

But the love of his studies was not smothered by this strenuous occupation. He not only perfected his knowledge of Latin and Greek, but before long blossomed forth as a writer.

More preferred the Greek authors to the Latin, and rightly so. The latter were mostly mere imitators of the former, and not always the happiest. In *Utopia*, Raphael Hythloday, who is the mouthpiece of More's opinions, is thus described: " He has not sailed as a seaman, but as a traveller, or rather a philosopher. This Raphael, who from his family carries the name of Hythloday, is not ignorant of the Latin tongue, but is eminently learned in the Greek, having applied himself more particularly to that than to the former, because he had given himself much to philosophy, in which he knew that the Romans have left us nothing that is valuable, except what is to be found in Seneca and Cicero."

Among the Greeks Plato was his favourite, and Plato's influence may be discerned from several passages in *Utopia* of which only the following need be quoted: " Therefore when I reflect on the constitution of the Utopians, and compare with them so many other nations ... I grow more favourable to Plato, and do not wonder that he resolved not to make any laws for such as would not submit to a community of all things."

In many ways Plato's *Republic* was the model for *Utopia*, and so far the latter is a genuine Humanistic work. This is not, however, to say that *Utopia*, or at least the constructive part of it, is a purely academic performance, a literary exercise, an attempt to describe the Platonic Republic in a new way. Nothing could be more erroneous. We shall see that *Utopia* was the product of the conditions under which More lived, that it possesses an essentially modern character, and that the resemblance to the Platonic Republic is only in externals.

Utopia was no mere scholastic exercise; it was designed to exert an influence on the nation's destiny. Moreover, its Humanist character is again revealed in the fact that it was not written in the vulgar tongue, but in a language which only a fraction of the nation understood— Latin.

More did not write exclusively in Latin, however. Humanism encouraged the classical Latin of Paganism, in contrast to the barbarous ecclesiastical Latin, but at the same time it was the first champion of national ideas and of national languages.

From Dante, Petrarch, and Boccaccio, the Humanists did more than revive classical Latin; they created a national prose, equally adapted to handling scientific and artistic material.

Thus More was not only one of the most elegant Latin scholars of his time; he was also " the father of English prose," as Sir James Mackintosh calls him. Before writing *Utopia*, More had composed works in English. In 1510 he translated from Latin into English a biography of the Humanist Pico of Mirandula, and in 1513 he wrote his famous *History of Richard III.*, which remained a fragment. This work was first published in 1543, after More's death, and at once became the classical account of the time which it described. From it is derived the unflattering portrait of Richard III. which Shakespeare has made immortal.

The rest of More's English works were composed subsequent to *Utopia*. They originated in the Reformation period, and are of an entirely polemical nature. In these treatises and dialogues More abandoned the Humanist standpoint, just as Hutten did in his German writings. Both employed the national language, not in the service of science and art, but of politics. They addressed themselves to the people, from whom as Humanists they had held proudly aloof.

3. *More on Education and the Position of Women.*

Both the Humanists and the Reformers employed and fostered the national languages for their own purposes, but the Humanists were exclusively concerned with the elevation of women, the natural sciences and the fine arts.

In respect of each of these matters More was in the front rank of the Humanists.

A letter which he wrote to Gunnell, his children's tutor, is particularly important for the light it throws on his views regarding the position of women. It contains the following passages: " In my view, learning united with virtue well deserves the preference to all the treasures of kings, but literary fame without virtue is nothing but a brilliant scandal. This applies specially to the learning of a courtisan. For in the case of the latter, any degree of knowledge is so rare and a secret reproach to men's idleness, that many love to attack her and to impute to literature what in reality is a defect of nature, believing that the faults of scholars stamp their own ignorance on virtue. If, however, a female person combines only a little knowledge with many laudable virtues, I esteem this above the wealth of Crœsus and the beauty of Helen. ... The difference between the sexes has nothing to do with the matter, for in the time of harvest it is all one whether the hand which sowed the seed belongs to a man or a woman. Both possess the same reason which distinguishes men from animals.   Both are therefore capable of those studies by which reason is perfected and fertilised, like a field over which the seed of good instruction has been sown.   If, however, as many contend who would debar women from study, the heritage of the female sex is infertile or brings forth weeds, this, in my opinion, is a reason to correct the faults of nature by diligent application and instruction in knowledge."

These principles were applied by More in the education of his three daughters and his foster-daughter, Margaret Giggs, whom he caused to receive a thorough instruction in the Humanist sciences.   Margaret, the eldest daughter, most resembled her father in spirit and disposition.   She acquired so much knowledge as to enjoy a notable reputation among the scholars of her time.   Her literary performances attracted widespread attention; Erasmus always wrote to her with the greatest deference, and once called her " Britannia's Jewel."   She spoke Greek and Latin fluently, translated Eusebius from Greek into Latin, and restored a mutilated passage in Cyprianus, performances which seem to us to-day as mere school exercises, but which at the beginning of the sixteenth century were regarded as prodigious and aroused general interest.   More was uncommonly fond of his daughter Margaret, and a letter from him to her is still preserved, in which he wished her, as the wife of his later biographer Roper, a happy issue to her impending confinement: may she bear a daughter like herself, which he would prefer to three youths.

Unfortunately she died in 1544, nine years after her father's execution, and in the lifetime of Henry VIII., when her father's memory was still under a cloud.   Had she survived to the days of the Catholic reaction, she would probably have given us a better biography of More than her husband was able to do.

In the excellent education which he gave his children,

More displayed the pedagogic talent common to all the great Utopists. The first socialists were primarily Utopists because they found that the human material of which the commonwealth was to be composed was too degraded and too undeveloped to permit of emancipation by their own efforts. The education of the people, not by prosecuting the class struggle, but by pedagogic methods, was thus a chief requirement of Utopian Socialists. Like Robert Owen, More was far in advance of his time as an educational reformer. As the former in his factory, so the latter in his family showed what brilliant results could be obtained by his methods. The means by which both obtained these results were benevolence, clemency, consistency, and mental superiority.

One of the educational principles which More followed is still honoured amongst us. In the above-quoted letter to Gunnell we read: " You say that to steer clear of vanity, which even men of great learning cannot conquer, is too great a task for children. But the harder it is to pull up this weed, the earlier we should nip it in the bud. The reason why this evil is so deeply rooted is that nurses, parents and teachers develop and foster it among children of tenderest years, for a child hardly does anything good but what it expects to be praised, and for this praise seeks to please most, even the worst."

More's amiable benevolence is extremely attractive even to-day. It is to be rated all the higher when we remember that the sixteenth century was one of the most cruel and bloodthirsty in the history of mankind. The age of Humanism was anything but the age of humanity. In the educational sphere it ushered in the age of the birch and of rote-learning. Erasmus relates that often after the common meal a schoolmaster would pick out a boy and hand him over for punishment to a rough bircher, who would never let a weak boy go until the sweat streamed down his face and the boy lay half dead at his feet. But the teacher would turn calmly to the scholars and say: " True he has done nothing, but he must be humiliated." Contrast this with More's educational principles.

4. *More's Relation to Art and Science.*

In human things More was more than a Humanist. Interest in art he shared with all Humanists, and he was devoted to music. The plastic arts also received a full meed of his attention. In this respect his relations with Hans Holbein the younger are of special interest. The latter came to England in 1526 with a letter of recommendation from Erasmus to More, who welcomed him with open arms. More kept Holbein in his house for a long time, in return for which Holbein decorated it with his paintings and painted More and his family. More later introduced Holbein at Court, and called Henry VIII.'s attention to the gifted painter.

Next to More's interest in art his predilection for the natural sciences is noteworthy.

Thomas More was one of the few who at the beginning of the sixteenth century were interested in investigating the laws of nature, and assigned a wider aim to the young natural sciences than the satisfaction of limited momentary needs. This is apparent from the part which he assigns to the natural sciences in his Utopian commonwealth.

We learn from More's biographers that he studied astronomy in addition to geometry, and he must have studied it to some purpose, as during the early part of his sojourn at Henry VIII.'s Court he was employed more as astronomer than as statesman. That his sole object was scientific investigation and not astrological predictions is obvious from his outbursts against the astrologers, whom he attacked not with moral indignation, but with his favourite weapon—ridicule. A number of his Latin epigrams were directed against the astrologers, the cleverest of which is one in which he mocks a stargazer who divines everything from the stars except that his wife has provided him with horns.

More was not only sceptical about astrologers; he also ridiculed the credulity of the pious and their taste for ghost stories. Next to Plato, his favourite writer was Lucian, the Heine of the expiring Roman world, to whom "nothing was holy," and who poured the stream of his wit over nascent Christianity and fashionable philosophers as well as over the old faiths. He read the writings of this sceptic, despite the warnings of pious friends, and defended him against them.

CHAPTER III

1. *More's Religiosity.*

ALTHOUGH More was a satirist and of a critical turn of mind, he did not, any more than the other English and German Humanists, attain to the sceptical outlook which marked Humanism in Italy and France. The economic development of the Teutonic countries was in the main behind that of the Latin countries, and the standard of intellectual life was lower. Pagan scepticism, the highest development of Humanism, was a mixture of contradictory elements. The scepticism of Humanism was partly defiance of traditional ecclesiastical ideas, partly the indolent indifference of a decadent class which mocked at the buoyant enthusiasm which it had felt in its own youth, but of which it had long grown incapable. Such a miserable type of scepticism was bound to repel the Northern " Barbarians," in whom the old mode of production had maintained some primitive energy and capacity for enthusiasm.

The freest minds of the North remained believing and pious. In fact, their faith was proportionate to their enthusiasm. We see this in the case of Hutten, Erasmus of Rotterdam, and More. With all his native energy of mind, the latter's piety sometimes verged on fanaticism and asceticism. There are indications of this in Erasmus' letter to Hutten, and numerous examples could be quoted from the works of his Catholic biographers.

104

Among the Italian Humanists More was most largely influenced by Pico della Mirandola, whose biography he translated from Latin into English, as we have seen. Pico, who was born in 1462 and died in 1494, was one of the few Italian Humanists who aimed at a moral and scientific purification of the Church and its doctrines, one of the few among them who had a certain spiritual affinity with the Reformers.

Pico regarded the Popes as hardly less dangerous than the Reformer Savonarola. The exploitation of the people was not jeopardised by the sceptical Humanists, whom the people did not understand, but by the pious who took the Church seriously, and whose ideas were in harmony with those of the people.

Pico attempted to purify the Christian doctrines by bringing them into line with the knowledge of his time. To accomplish this, he not only studied the Pagan world of Greece, but was also one of the first Christians to learn Hebrew with scientific thoroughness in order to track the secrets of Christianity through the mystical philosophy of Kabbala. The results of his studies were set out in his *Nine Hundred Principles*, where, among other things, he denied eternal punishment and the presence of Christ in the Sacrament. Had Pico been a proper reformer— that is, an agitator—he would have been burnt for those principles. As he was only a man of science, Pope Innocent VIII. contented himself with prohibiting the work.

This semi-heretic Pico was More's ideal.

2. *More an Opponent of Clericalism.*

More's interest in Pico shows that he was not so priest-ridden as both Catholic and Protestant clergy would like to make out. It is true that in his youth he entered a

Cartesian monastery and passed some time there in pious exercises. The priest Stapleton is obliged to admit that More abandoned his intention of becoming a monk, as "the priests of his time had lapsed from their former discipline and lost their pious enthusiasm."

More retracted nothing from his censure of the priesthood. He could ridicule the monks as much as any other Humanist.

Listen, for instance, to the following passage from the first book of *Utopia*. Raphael Hythloday is describing a meal at Cardinal Morton's, at which a jester and a friar are present. The talk turns on what should be done with beggars who become incapable of work owing to old age or other causes. The jester says that he never gives alms to a beggar. "They now know me so well that they let me pass because they hope for nothing, no more than if I were a priest. . . . But I would have a law made for sending all these beggars to monasteries, the men to the Benedictines to be lay brothers, and the women to be nuns." The Cardinal smiled and treated the proposal as a jest, the others taking it seriously. But a brother theologian was so amused by the joke about priests and nuns that, although otherwise a grave man, he began to jest, and said to him: "This will not deliver you from all beggars, except you take care of us friars." "That is done already," answered the fool, "for the Cardinal has provided for you, by what he proposed for restraining vagabonds, and setting them to work, for I know no vagabonds like you." A quarrel ensues between the friar and the jester, in which More makes the friar look so foolish that he draws upon himself general laughter. Of course, the friar ends by threatening the fool with the wrath of God: "For if the many mockers of Elisha, who was but one bald man, felt the effect of his zeal, what will become of one mocker of so many friars, among whom there are so many bald men ? We have likewise a Bull, by which all that jeer us are excommunicated."

The Cardinal changed the subject, and put a stop to the friar's railing, and thus ends the episode which in a few words holds up to ridicule the stupidity, laziness, and greed of the monks.

The ridicule of our " Catholic Martyr " was not confined to the lower clergy; even the bishops came in for their share; notably the one whom More calls Posthumus is the target of his wit in his epigrams.

In one of these More expresses his delight that the said Posthumus has been made a bishop, for whereas bishops are usually appointed haphazard, without any regard for their qualifications, it would seem that this one had been chosen with special care. A worse and more stupid bishop could scarcely have been found among thousands.

The next epigram says of the same bishop: " He is fond of quoting the text, ' The letter kills, but the spirit maketh to live,' but Posthumus is much too ignorant for any letter to kill him, and had it done so, he had no spirit to be quickened."

Even the Pope only seemed an ordinary mortal to More.

In More's house, and under his encouragement, Erasmus wrote *The Praise of Folly*, in which More took great delight. The manuscript was secretly taken away by one of its author's friends, probably by More himself, and sent to Paris, where it was printed in 1511, and seven editions appeared in a few months.

This book was an extremely bold and flippant satire on the whole of contemporary society, especially on monkery and the Papacy. It was therefore put on the index of prohibited books. There is no reason for thinking that More ever regretted his share in the work.

But we do not need such indirect proofs of More's attitude towards the Papacy. We have some of his utterances during the time when the Reformation was beginning and the struggle against Protestantism should have drawn him closer to the Papacy. Yet he wrote, in his *Confutation of Tyndall's Answer* (1532), that a general council is above the Pope, whom it exhorts and punishes, and can even depose if he prove incorrigible.

When the Reformation began, Henry VIII. declared emphatically against it and in favour of the Pope. He even published a book against Luther, which was published under his name in 1521, but, as often happens in such cases, it was written by other people.

Although More was regarded as its author, he had only a small share in the book. When Henry VIII. broke away from the Papacy, this book was a source of annoyance. The author of his book had now become a traitor.

Amongst other charges brought against More when he resigned his position as Lord Chancellor in 1532, was that " by his subtle sinister slights most unnaturally procuring and provoking the King to set forth a book of the Assertion of the Seven Sacraments and maintenance of the Pope's authority had caused him, to his dishonour, throughout all Christendom, to put a sword in the Pope's hand to fight against himself."

The comical aspect of the moral indignation of the poor misguided King is that for ten years he had passed as the author of the book, accepting all the praise bestowed upon it. Now the book was turned against More, and he must take the punishment. More answered, as Roper tells us:

" My Lords, these terrors be arguments for children and not for me. But to answer to that wherewith you do chiefly burden me, I believe the King's highness of his honour will never lay to my charge, for none is there that can in that point say in my excuse more than his highness himself, who right well knoweth that I was never procurer or Counsellor of his Majesty thereunto; but after it was finished, by his Grace's appointment and consent of the makers of the same, I was only a sorter out and placer of the principal matters therein contained. Wherein when I found the Pope's authority highly advanced and with strong arguments mightily defended, I said unto his Grace, I must put your Highness in remembrance of one thing, and that is this: the Pope, as your Grace knoweth, is a prince as you are, and in league with all other Christian princes. It may hereafter so fall out that your Grace and he may vary upon some points of the league, whereupon may grow breach of amity and war between you both. I think it best therefore that the place be amended and his authority more slenderly touched. Nay, quoth his Grace, that shall it not; we are so much bounden unto the See of Rome that we cannot do too much honour to it. Then did I further put him in remembrance of the Statute of Premunire, whereby a good part of the Pope's pastoral cure here was wasted away. To that answered his Highness: Whatsoever impediment be to the contrary, we will set forth the authority to the uttermost; for we received from that See of Rome our crown imperial, which till his Grace with his own mouth told it to me, I never heard of before."

The charge broke down. Neither Henry himself nor anyone else could contest the accuracy of More's statements. We may therefore accept them. It is evident from them that More was far from cherishing a slavish reverence for the Papacy. He regarded it, as we shall show in the next chapter, as an international cohesive force, without which Christendom would dissolve into a chaos of mutually hostile nations. Nevertheless he defended the rights of single nations, as of the whole Church, against the Pope, who in his eye was nothing more than the removable president of Christianity.

3. *More's Religious Tolerance.*

How freely More thought about religious matters may be inferred from the ideal religion which he ascribed to his Utopians. We shall become acquainted with them in the third part of our book. Here we would mention a characteristic which placed More far above the Catholicism as well as the Protestantism of his time, and which he shared with few of his contemporaries: his religious tolerance. He proclaimed it not only before the Reformation in his *Utopia*, but also in the midst of the fiercest struggles between Protestants and Catholics, when the fires of the stake were everywhere reddening the sky.

Stapleton finds it very strange that a Catholic saint should receive a Lutheran in his house. Simon Grynæus, a pupil and disciple of Melanchthon, came to England to collect materials for his translations of the works of the Greek Neoplatonic philosopher Proclus. In this undertaking he received so much support from More, then Lord Chancellor, that he dedicated the translation to More's son, John, as More was dead before the book was ready. This dedication, which throws a strong light on More's character, read as follows:

"Your glorious father, who by virtue of his position as of his distinguished talents, was then the first man in the kingdom, procured me, an unknown individual, access to many public and private institutions and found a place for me at his table. But more than this; he observed with all good nature that my religious opinions deviated in not a few points from his. Yet his solicitude remained the same, and he arranged to meet all my expenses out of his own pocket."

This took place more than a decade after Luther's declaration of war against Rome.

Yet Protestant and Liberal writers have sought to brand More as a persecutor of heretics. The proof of More's alleged intolerance, apart from unfounded assertions, lies in his self-composed epitaph: *Furibus, homicidis, hæreticis molestus.* This juxtaposition is not very flattering for the heretic, but the *molestus* does not necessarily imply that heresy is to be put down by force. By tolerance More meant that an opponent was not to be silenced by force. But he did not regard it as intolerance to exert his whole intellectual strength to impose his own convictions and shatter those of his opponent. He was far too combative in his nature to ask for quarter from an opponent, nor did he feel called upon to blunt his own weapons.

To what extent More persecuted heretics he tells us himself in his *Apology*, written in 1533, after resigning his position as Lord Chancellor. His statements bear the impress of truth, and are confirmed by independent testimony, so far as this is available. They therefore deserve to be believed, because More had no interest in hiding the truth, and a deliberate lie was foreign to his nature.

Soon after composing his *Apology* he went to his death because he would utter no lie.

We quote the following passage: " When I was first of the King's Council and after his under treasurer, and in the time while I was Chancellor of his Duchy of Lancaster of this realm, it was mightily meetly well known what manner of favour I bare toward the clergy and that as I loved and honoured the good, so was not remiss nor slack in providing for the correction of those that were nought noxious to good people and slanderous to their own order. Which sort of priests and religious running out of religion and falling to theft and murder had at my hands so little favour that there was no man that had any meddling with them into whose hands they were more loth to come." He then proceeds to discuss the assertion that he was a persecutor of heretics. "Divers of them (the Lutherans) have said that of such as were in my house while I was Chancellor I used to examine them with torments, causing them to be bounden to a tree in my garden and there piteously beaten. And this tale had some of those good brethren so caused to be blown about that a right worshipful friend of mine did of late tell that he had heard much speaking thereof. What can not these brethren say that can be so shameless to say thus. For of very truth, albeit that for a great robbery, or a heinous murder, or sacrilege in a church, with carrying away the pire with the blessed sacrament, or villainously casting it out, I caused sometime such things to be done by some officers of the Marshalsea or of some other prisons. Yet though I so did in thieves, murderers and robbers of churches, notwithstanding also that heretics be yet much worse, I never did cause any such thing to be done to any of them in all my life, except only twain." These two cases were described in detail. One case related to a youth in More's service who tried to teach another youth in his house to make fun of the sacrament. More dealt with him as boys are usually dealt with. The other case related to a mad fellow who had once been in an asylum and whose chief pleasure consisted in attending mass and raising shouts to the scandal of the congregation. More once had him arrested by a constable, as he was passing the house. He was tied to a tree and whipped. These two cases were tolerably harmless according to the standards of the time, when witches and heretics were burnt out of hand.

More continues: "And of all that ever came in my hand for heresy, saving as I said the sure keeping of them, as help me God, had never any of them any stripe or stroke given them so much as a fillip on the forehead. . . . Touching heretics, I hate that vice of theirs and not their persons, and very fain would I that the one were destroyed and the other saved."

More also referred to the complaint of his opponents that he could not forbear to raise a laugh when treating of serious things. That is so: More was no preacher on the lines of the newer Catholicism. However he tried to keep a straight face in his polemical religious writings, cheerfulness would come breaking through. Most amusing are some of the passages in his *Supplication of Souls* (1529), a reply to the pamphlet *Supplication of Beggars*, which called on Henry VIII. to confiscate the pious endowments for the benefit of the workless proletariat.

Fiske, the author, demanded that the monks should be driven from their monasteries, set to work under the lash, and married, thus increasing the production and population of the country at the same time. "Think of it," says More, "requesting the King to have the monks robbed, chained, whipped, and—married. What the author thinks of marriage may be inferred from his putting it last in the category of evils."

This is the style of More's "theological" treatises. It is true that towards the end of his life they became less serene and sometimes bore an ecstatic and fanatical character, and that he said in them things which contradict his former principles, as expressed, for instance, in *Utopia*.

An investigation as to how much a change came about belongs rather to the realm of psychology than of history. For us they have merely a pathological interest, as we are concerned only with More the thinker and socialist. Once we understand it, More's theological literature explains clearly enough why he elected to take the Catholic and not the Protestant side.

Having made this decision, all that followed was the

8

natural consequence of this step.   The reasons, however, which induced him to oppose Protestantism were not of a dogmatic or theological, but of a political and economic nature; partly the same reasons which moved Humanism generally to fight on the Catholic side, and which we have already discussed.

But owing to local and personal influences these reasons assumed a peculiar character in the case of More.

CHAPTER IV

MORE AS POLITICIAN

1. *The Political Condition of England at the Beginning of the Sixteenth Century.*

WE have already described the general political situation of Europe in the fifteenth and sixteenth centuries. A few words will suffice to indicate the special aspects of this situation in England.

At the end of the fifteenth century the two most power, ful of the medieval estates, the Nobility and the Church—were completely subjugated by the Crown. The tendency of the general development, which was to weaken both these estates, was accentuated in England by a number of special circumstances. The power of the feudal nobility received a formidable blow from the Wars of the Roses. The English Barons, as predatory as their forefathers, had sought to acquire spoil and land and people first in the Holy Land and then in France. When these sources of plunder were stopped up, the English nobles were perforce thrown back on quarrelling with each other for the only objects of exploitation that remained: the land and people of England.

In 1453 Calais was all of France that was still in the hands of the English. The whole mob of noble English exploiters, who up to a few years before were still deriving large gains from the conquered countries, suddenly found themselves crowded within the narrow confines of their Motherland.

There was a redundancy of exploiters. The proceeds were insufficient to permit them to continue living the extravagant lives which the exploitation of France had accustomed them to. The natural consequences of this redundancy was a " struggle for existence," the division of the English nobility into two hostile factions, which, under the pretext of defending the claim of the House of York or that of the House of Lancaster to the Throne of England, slaughtered and plundered each other. The Wars of the Roses were a contest for the right to the Throne about as much as the struggle between protectionists and free traders is a battle for the rights of the poor man.

In reality they were a struggle between two exploiting factions for the object of plunder, carried on with immense bitterness and cruelty. Both parties adopted the attitude of granting no pardon, and any noble who escaped death on the battlefield fell victim to the axe of the executioner of the momentary victorious party.

In this fearful carnage, which lasted a generation (from 1452, when the French possessions were finally lost, until 1485), nearly the whole of the nobility perished, and their landed property fell to the king, who created therewith a new nobility possessing neither the power nor the prerogatives of the feudal caste. True, the great English landowners were once more to become a power which could defy the monarchy and make it dependent upon them, but this was not yet the case in the time of Thomas More, who was born seven years before the close of the Civil War. The higher nobles of More's time were nearly all creatures of the monarchy, owing their possessions to the reigning king or his father, and therefore being wholly dependent upon him.

The clergy, like the nobles, had also been degraded into being servants of the monarchy. Perhaps no other monarchy in Europe had been so dependent upon the Papacy as was England after the Norman Conquest.

The Normans had won the country with the assistance of the Church, in return for which the victorious Norman Duke William the Conqueror, who now became England's king, acknowledged himself as a fief of the Pope. Later, in the year 1213, John Lackland was obliged to accept his kingdom from the Pope against an annual payment of 1,000 marks.

The Norman feudal monarchy of England had every reason to assist the aggrandisement of the Papacy so long as the English nobles might hope that the Crusades would unlock for them the treasury houses of the East. As the prospects of this became increasingly slender towards the end of the thirteenth century, the exploitation of France became of paramount interest for the English knights and barons, and at the same time English merchants became interested in the acquirement of French possessions with which they could drive a prosperous trade, unhindered by duties and other obstacles. In the contest with France, however, the Pope was not an ally, but an opponent of the English, France having made him wholly her tool in the fourteenth century. This hostility brought to a head the anti-papal sentiment in England more rapidly than in the other non-Romance countries; it strengthened in all lands exploited by the Papacy the influences which since the fourteenth century had been increasingly striving for independence of Rome. In England, as later in Germany, this hostility to the Papacy assumed two mutually antagonistic shapes, according to the classes in which it was embodied: on the one hand a democratic form, proceeding from the peasants, the artisans, and sometimes the lesser nobles; on the other hand a monarchical form, proceeding from the monarchy and its creatures and the merchants.

The first tendency favoured the doctrines of Wicliff and gave rise to the sect of Lollards.

The monarchical tendency was satisfied, without disturbing the dogmas of the Church, to impose considerable legal restrictions upon the Papacy, which crippled its power to exploit.

As early as 1360 Parliament passed laws to this end. In 1390 every Englishman was forbidden, under penalty of losing his property and life, to accept any benefice from a foreigner or to send money out of the country. And this measure was reinforced by the Statute of Premunire, which has become a basic law of the English Constitution. It rested with the kings if and how far this law should be enforced. By virtue of it they became almost entirely independent of the Papacy, upon which they could exert strong pressure by threatening to strictly enforce the Statute of Premunire. But the days were long past when the national clergy, independent of the Pope, could defy the King.

They could not escape dependence upon the Papacy without falling into dependence upon the monarchy. The clergy became the servants of the king in the degree that the Pope's power in England declined.

Nor did the Turkish danger assist the Papacy to recover its power in England, which of all countries in Europe had least to fear from the Turks.

Thus it fell out that in More's time the English nobility and clergy were the submissive servants of the monarchy, to which they imparted an absolute power such as it then possessed in no other country of Europe.

With the rise of the monarchy, however, the burghers and peasants came to the fore. We have already shown how the peasants substantially improved their position in Europe generally at the end of the thirteenth and the beginning of the fourteenth centuries. Serfdom was vanishing, personal service was in many places entirely abolished, and often replaced by money taxes, a change which also offered many advantages to the landlords. The labour of paid hands, of wage workers, took the place of serf labour. But the number of people compelled to take service for wages was then but small, and wages were high. Slight causes were sufficient to effect a rapid rise in wages. A number of circumstances, such as the ravages of the Black Death, which broke out in England in 1348; the rise of new industries, which attracted considerable labour power to the towns—as the Norwich woollen industry in the fourteenth century—or which created a domestic industry in the country and thereby reduced the number of available wage workers; distant wars, which absorbed soldiers—all this brought about a general rise of 50 per cent., and for a time much more, in the wages of the English workers during the second half of the fourteenth century.

The landlords fell into despair. They tried to make the labourers work and to reduce wages by Act of Parliament. The first of these statutes of labourers was passed in 1349. But the landlords were not satisfied with these laws. They sought to reimpose the yoke of serfdom directly upon workers and peasants.

Finally the oppression became intolerable. Workers and peasants rose under Wat Tyler in 1381. The rebellion had no direct success. Its leader was treacherously slain, the insurgents were disbanded, their ringleaders executed, and Lollardry was cruelly persecuted. But the rebellion gave the landlords a salutary fright; they desisted from their attempts to coerce peasants and workers. The civil wars of the fifteenth century broke up feudalism completely.

Thus a defiant and sturdy race of free peasants developed in England. It was these peasants who made England's army formidable from the fourteenth to the sixteenth century, and against whose resistance the flower of France was shattered, as were later the Cavaliers of the Stuarts.

They formed a body of men which could be very dangerous to the monarchical power if a class should exist which knew how to use them for this purpose. In the absence of affiliations with another class, the peasant was not dangerous; he had no political or material aspirations, and his interest did not extend much further than the bounds of his community, hardly beyond those of his county. Left at peace within these bounds, he was content.

However free the English peasant might have felt under Henry VII. or Henry VIII.—that is, in More's time— he offered no obstacle to kingly absolutism, towards which his feelings were indifferent if not friendly, as he discerned in absolutism a bulwark against the invasions of the large landowners, which were beginning in More's time, and which we shall deal with later.

No more than from the strengthening of the peasant class did the monarchy suffer any loss through the rapid increase in the power of the burghers. Of the two sections which composed it, the handicraftsmen were then an unruly element, defiant and self-conscious and never shirking a fight. Next to the peasants, they supplied the most numerous recruits for Lollardry. But like the peasant, the artisan, or at least the artisan of the country towns, lived and worked much more in his community than in the State, and however rebellious and stubborn in his local affairs, he exercised no permanent influence upon national affairs. Moreover, in More's age guild handicraft was already on the decline in many country towns, and its decay was so rapid that the Protector Somerset could proceed to confiscate guild property for the Crown, just as Henry VIII. had confiscated Church property. And this at a time when the foundations of the sanctity of the modern form of property were being laid.

In any case this confiscation was only carried out in the country towns, not in London. Nobody dared to touch the guilds of this city. In More's time the citizens of London were a power for which the English kings had more respect than for the Church, the nobles, the peasants, and the country towns. The centralising tendency of trade had nowhere asserted itself so early and so widely as in France and England, the two States which were the earliest to become national States.

Paris and London were the first towns to make the whole economic life of their countries tributary to them, and their masters were the actual masters of the country.

The merchants possessed the greatest power in London. London was primarily a commercial city, and there England's trade, considerable even in More's time, was centred.

In the thirteenth century the Hanseatic League undertook the largest part of the English carrying trade, and London was the site of one of its most flourishing factories, the Steelyard; in the fifteenth century English ships sailed to France and the Netherlands, to Portugal and Morocco; they penetrated to the Baltic and there started a bitter competition with the Hanseatic League; in this direction one trading company, the Merchant Adventurers, was particularly active. The development of the fisheries also fostered the expansion of the Mercantile Marine.

English mariners became ever bolder and more enterprising, venturing farther and farther into uncharted seas. Trade and the whale drew them to Iceland; and in the era of discoveries they were to make discoveries in the North Sea, which, while not so profitable as those of the Spaniards and Portuguese, required quite as much daring and seamanship as the latter.

A few years after More's death they were to find the way to Archangel on the northern coast of Russia, and in 1497 John Cabot of Bristol, sailing in English ships, discovered Labrador and thus reached the American continent almost fourteen months before Columbus.

Important as were these discoveries and the bold enterprising spirit to which they were due for the subsequent commercial greatness of England, in More's day they had merely a symptomatic significance. England's chief trade was then carried on with much nearer countries; the wool trade with the Netherlands was its most important part.

Wool-combing had early—in the tenth century—developed in the Netherlands, for which it had created great wealth. Up to the seventeenth century, however, there were only two countries in Europe which exported wool: England and Spain. English wool was much better than the Spanish and within easier reach of the Netherlands. Consequently, England actually monopolised the wool trade with the Netherlands, just as in the eighteen sixties the Southern States of the American Union monopolised the supply to England of the cotton that was indispensable for the textile industry. England's wealth therefore grew with the wealth of the Netherlands, or rather the wealth of the wool-growing great landowners, the merchants, and the monarchs of England. The growth in the wealth of the former had up to More's time been checked partly by the civil wars and the devastations and confiscations which followed in their wake, partly by the absence of a proletariat, a reserve army of workless, to keep down wages. Not until More's time was any effort made to remove this deplorable lack of poverty in the interest of national prosperity. Henceforth the great landowners received their proper share in the profits of the wool monopoly. Previously the lion's share had fallen to the merchants and the monarchs. The export duty on wool then formed one of the most fertile sources of the revenue of the English kings, and was one of the firmest supports of absolutism. The more trade developed, the stronger became the king's power in the country, but the more, too, the king was obliged to serve the interests of commerce.

The Tudors, whose rule began with Henry VII. and ended with Elizabeth, perceived quite early that the interests of commerce were also theirs, and therefore fostered trade generally as far as they could. Tyrannically as they reigned, the London citizens, the decisive power in the realm next to the monarchy, tolerated their rule; the citizens of London lived almost entirely by trade, directly or indirectly, and so long as trade flourished they had no cause for rebellion.

Thus the Tudor rule encountered no obstacle; it was the most absolute that has ever existed in England.

It must not be imagined that the English bourgeoisie was in a state of abjection on this account. It was fully aware of its strength, and did not shirk opposing the monarchy, when the latter's policy was inimical to its interests. And the absolute rule of the Tudors would not have lasted over a hundred years if they had not for the most part known exactly how far they might go and effected a timely retreat before the people on the occasions when they overshot the mark.

The resistance and freedom-loving sentiments of the people, above all of London, was the sole impediment to the power of the Tudors.

Their parliaments were impotent. Since the thirteenth century representatives of the towns, as well as of the nobility and clergy, had been summoned to Parliament, of course, merely for the purpose of compelling the towns to make monetary grants. Meanwhile, as the wealth of the towns grew, the power of their representatives and their influence on legislation increased. It was a peculiarity of the English Parliament that, in the fourteenth century, the representatives of the lower nobility separated from the higher nobility, who henceforth formed the Upper House, together with the higher dignitaries of the Church, and united with the representatives of the towns and constituted the Lower House. The power of Parliament, of course, depended on the classes that stood behind it and upon their unity. Where two hostile parties held the balance, the king had an easy task. Until the seventeenth century, however, the power of Parliament in its contests with the ruling power was less than that of the classes it represented, as members of Parliament were accessible to personal influences. The middle classes could not be bribed or intimidated, but their representatives could; while the king could have members of Parliament who displeased him executed for high treason.

If a king yielded to Parliament, it was not out of regard for its rights, but out of concern for the power of those whose interests it represented.

Provided they remained on good terms with the people, the Tudors had no need to propitiate their parliaments.

Impotent, subject to personal influences, composed for the greater part of noble and spiritual creatures of the king, the parliaments of Tudor times were indeed the most servile in English history. They left legislation wholly to the monarchy and willingly discharged the office of executioner required of them. Only on one point were they obstinate, frequently compelling the kings to yield because they had the masses behind them, and that was the question of granting supplies.

All the conditions above described fostered a strange apparent contradiction. Nowhere in Europe was the absolute power of the monarchy greater than in the England of More's time, and perhaps in no country were the freedom-loving sentiments and self-consciousness of the citizens more strongly developed than there.

2. *More as Monarchist and Opponent of Tyranny.*

More was the child of the conditions described above. The contradiction referred to was therefore reflected in his writings. Owing to his enthusiastic temperament, he perhaps reveals it more clearly than anyone else. He absorbed with avidity the doctrine of the Humanists that a prince was really necessary, but he should be the servant of philosophers. He extended this to include the people, and what with others was merely a literary flourish was his firm conviction. He hated tyranny as only an Englishman can hate it, and yet he was convinced of the necessity of the monarchy. He held it right to depose the king if he acted contrary to the people's interests, but only in order to put a better king in his place.

This, shortly, is his political standpoint. It may best be elucidated by a short description of More's political thought and actions.

His first political expressions are to be found in his epigrams. One of them deals with " The good and the bad prince ":

" What is a good prince? A sheepdog, who keeps away the wolves? And a bad prince? The wolf himself."

Another is entitled, " The difference between a tyrant and a prince."

" How is a legitimate king distinguished from a loathsome tyrant? The tyrant holds his subjects for his slaves, the king regards them as his children."

The distinction reminds one of the fiction of constitutionalists, who hold that while the king reigns he does not govern. More needed this fiction to reconcile his theoretical conviction as to the necessity of monarchy with the hatred he felt for the tyranny of the reigning king, who was then Henry VII.

The kind of ideas which filled his mind may be inferred from his translating Lucian's dialogue, *The Tyrannicide*, from Greek into Latin, and composing a reply thereto.

It has been sought by More's clerical biographers to represent his preoccupation with such themes as a mere academical interest, but the Catholic Audin, who wrote a commentary to the French translation of Stapleton's biography, published in Paris in 1849, was obliged to admit that *The Tyrannicide* is a political confession of faith. More hated despotism, and did not believe in divine right; he is ready to acquit anyone who rebels against a bad prince.

3. *More as Representative of the London Merchants.*

More soon had occasion to prove that his " manly pride before the prince's throne " was more than a theoretical flourish. At the age of twenty-six he was elected to the Parliament convened by Henry VII., in order to obtain legal pretexts for plundering the people. The late Parliament of 1496-97 had without demur voted two fifteenths on account of the threatened war with Scotland. The fifteenths was a property tax of a specific amount, paid by the counties, towns, and holdings, as also by the clergy. In 1500 the yield of a fifteenth was estimated at £37,930.

The king's avarice grew with the complaisancy of Parliament. He demanded three fifteenths from the Parliament of 1504, in which More sat. The money was partly for the dowry of his daughter Margaret, who was marrying the King of Scotland, partly for a contribution on the occasion of the knighthood of his son Arthur.

To appreciate the shameless character of the demand, it should be remembered that the knighthood contribution was derived from the feudal constitution and had long fallen into disuse; it had last been granted in the middle of the fourteenth century, when the Black Prince was made a knight. Moreover, Arthur had died in 1502.

Yet Parliament did not seem reluctant to concede the demand. The Bill had already passed two readings when " at the last debate More made such argument and reasons thereagainst that the King's demand thereby was clean overthrown; so that one of the King's privy chamber, named Master Tiler, being present thereat, brought word to the King out of the Parliament House that a beardless boy had disappointed all his purpose," as Roper tells us. It seems, however, that Henry's demand was not entirely rejected, but the amount was reduced.

As may be imagined, Henry VII. was enraged at the young opposition leader. First of all he addressed himself to the father, as the son possessed no property which he could have confiscated. He imprisoned old John More in the Tower, and fined him £100, but this did not satisfy his revenge. The young politician was obliged to withdraw from public life and remain in hiding to escape the tyrant's anger. This was probably the time of More's sojourn in a monastery and his intention of becoming a monk. More also contemplated emigrating at the time.

After a time the King forgot " the beardless boy," but More was obliged to be cautious and keep away from Parliament. That he was not idle at this time is evident from the fact that immediately after Henry VII.'s death in 1509 he was appointed Under Sheriff of London, a promotion which proved that he had gained some reputation as a lawyer. In this office he must have quickly acquired the confidence of his fellow citizens, and at the same time gained a profound insight into the economic situation of the country, for we soon find him entrusted with important missions as the representative of the London merchants. Roper tells us: "For his learning, wisdom, knowledge and experience, men had such estimation that before he came to the service of King Henry VIII., at the suit and instance of the English merchants, he was by the King's consent made twice ambassador in certain great causes between them and the merchants of the Steelyard." The conclusion of this passage is based on a misunderstanding, as it was not until a later date that More was deputed to compose quarrels with the Hanseatic League.

The first of these commissions was entrusted to More in the year 1515. Of this More tells us in the first book of *Utopia:* "Henry the Eighth, the unconquered King of England, a prince adorned with all the virtues that become a great monarch, having some differences of no small consequence with Charles, the most serene prince of Castile, sent me into Flanders, as his ambassador, for treating and composing matters between them."

Prince Charles, the later Emperor Charles V., as heir of the German Emperor Maximilian and a boy of three, was betrothed to the French Princess Claudia, then two years old. A change in diplomatic relations led to the rupture of this betrothal, and Charles was betrothed with Mary, daughter of Henry VII. of England, in the year 1506, but in 1514 Maximilian found it useful for the purposes of an alliance with France to betroth Charles again with a French princess, the younger sister of his first fiancée. The father of the first and third fiancées, Louis XII., married the second discarded fiancée, the English Princess Mary.

This series of betrothals is typical of the absolutism of

the time of More.   Small scattered States were then welded
into larger States by marriages, and nobody was accounted
a statesman who was not a skilful marriage broker.

Henry VIII. was, of course, much displeased at Maximilian's treachery.   In 1515 Charles assumed the government of the Netherlands, and Henry promptly sought
to injure him by inducing Parliament to forbid the export
of wool to the Netherlands.   Soon, however, Henry made
his peace with Charles, and moreover the prohibition of
the export of wool was as inconvenient for the English
merchants as for the Hollanders.   More was sent to re-
open this trade.   His mission was attended with complete
success, and consequently he was sent to Calais in 1517
on a similar expedition, in order to settle disputes between
English and French merchants.

More proved so versatile and his reputation in London
was so high that Henry had every reason to attract him
to Court, but More held aloof.   He even refused a pension
which the King offered him, fearing he would thereby
forfeit the confidence of his fellow citizens.

He was resolved to champion civic freedom, should
strife break out between the London citizens and the King.

In fact, he had no cause to be pleased with Henry VIII.
Henry VII. had been a miser, hoarding money, and bleed-
ing the people whenever and wherever he could.   His son
was amiable and generous, encouraging trade and the arts
by his luxurious habits, a friend of the new sciences and
of Humanism; in short, a liberal Crown Prince according
to the ideas of his time.   Universal joy greeted him when
he ascended the throne.

More, too, hoped that a prince had now come who would
submit to the guidance of philosophers, and be a father
to his people, and not a slaveholder.

The first acts of Henry VIII.'s government were also
calculated to make him popular; above all, the execution

of Empson and Dudley, the two zealous ministers of Henry VII.

Soon, however, Henry's policy disclosed a less popular side. He joined the so-called "Holy League" against France (1512) and took part in the war against France, which lasted until 1514, costing England much money and bringing little glory and no advantage.

Henry had allowed himself to be made the cat's-paw of other people, in particular, the Catholic Ferdinand of Aragon, who was well pleased with the "Holy War" for the protection of the "Holy Father."

To the costs of the war was added the expense of the upkeep of a luxurious court and a mania for building. Henry built fifty palaces, and was so impatient for their completion that the workers were hardly allowed to rest. He well deserved the fame of being one of the first in England to introduce night work and Sunday work on a large scale.

The greed of the spendthrift was worse than that of the miser. There was no limit to the taxes, and even the poorest labourers were burdened. One of the new fiscal laws enacted that workers with an annual wage of £2 must pay one shilling, those earning £1 per annum sixpence, and those earning less, fourpence.

Moreover, there was the favourite device of debasing the currency, which, of course, could only yield temporary gains, but proved very useful when debts had to be paid.

4. *The Political Criticism of "Utopia."*

Such a prince as Henry VIII. was not the "sheepdog who protected his flock from the wolves," but the wolf himself. More felt profoundly disillusioned, and in this frame of mind wrote *Utopia*. In the second book he describes how happy a State could be if it were rationally organised and governed.

The first book shows how badly States were governed in reality, and what crimes stained Henry's reign in particular. This book is an important document for the glimpses it gives of the economic and political situation at the beginning of the sixteenth century and for the light it throws on More as a politician. We must therefore consider it closely.

In estimating the book we must no more be misled by the homage paid to the King than we should judge the materialists of the eighteenth century by the reverence they occasionally accorded to Christianity.

In both cases the art of the critics on the opposition side consisted in suggesting that the reader should read between the lines the opposite of what they purported to convey.

Thus in *Utopia* More assigned the championship of his standpoint to Raphael Hythloday, while he introduces himself as a critic of his ideas. Not what More says, but what Hythloday says, is important. More relates how he met Raphael in Bruges on the occasion of his mission. He and his friend Peter Giles implore Raphael to enter the King's service. The latter refuses, and gives his reasons in detail. These passages well deserve quotation.

" I wonder, Raphael, how it comes that you enter into no king's service, for I am sure there are none to whom you would not be very acceptable; for your learning and knowledge, both of men and things, is such, that you would not only entertain them very pleasantly, but be of great use to them, by the examples you could set before them, and the advices you could give them; and by this means you would both serve your own interest, and be of great use to all your friends." "As for my friends," answered he, " I need not be much concerned, having already done for them all that was incumbent on me; for when I was not only in good health, but fresh and young, I distributed that among my kindred and friends which other people do not part with till they are old and sick; when they then unwillingly give that which they can enjoy no longer themselves, I think my friends ought to rest contented with this, and not to expect that for their sakes I should enslave myself to any king whatsoever." "Soft and fair," said Peter; "I do not mean that you should be a slave to any king, but only that you should assist them, and be useful to them." "The change of the word," said he, "does not alter the matter." "But term it as you will," replied Peter, "I do not see any other way in which you can be so useful, both in private to your friends, and to the public, and by which you can make your own condition happier." "Happier," answered Raphael; "is that to be compassed in a way so abhorrent to my genius? Now I live as I will, to which I believe few courtiers can pretend. And there are so many that court the favour of great men, that there will be no great loss if they are not troubled either with me or with others of my temper." Upon this, said More, "I perceive, Raphael, that you neither desire wealth nor greatness; and indeed I value and admire a man much more than I do any of the great men in the world. Yet I think you would do what would well become so generous and philosophical a soul as yours is, if you would apply your time and thoughts to public affairs, even though you may happen to find it a little uneasy to yourself: and this you can never do with so much advantage, as by being taken into the counsel of some great prince, and putting him on noble and worthy actions, which I know you would do if you were in such a post; for the springs both of good and evil flow from the prince, over a whole nation, as from a lasting fountain. So much learning as you have, even without practice in affairs, or so great a practice as you have had, without any other learning, would render you a very fit counsellor to any king whatsoever." "You are doubly mistaken," said he, "Mr. More, both in your opinion of me, and in the judgment you make of things: for as I have not that capacity that you fancy I have, so, if I had it, the public would not be one jot the better, when I had sacrificed my quiet to it. For most princes apply themselves more to affairs of war than to the useful arts of peace; and in these I neither have any knowledge, nor do I much desire it: they are generally more set on acquiring new kingdoms, right or wrong, than on governing well those they possess. And among the ministers of princes, there are none that are not so wise as to need no assistance, or at least that do not think themselves so wise, that they imagine they need none; and if they court any, it is only those for whom the prince has much personal favour, whom by their fawnings and flatteries they endeavour to fix to their own interests: and indeed Nature has so made us, that we all love to be flattered, and to please ourselves with our own notions. The old crow loves his young, and the ape her cubs. Now if in such a Court, made up of persons who envy all others, and only admire themselves, a person should but propose anything that he had either read in history, or observed in his travels, the rest would think that the reputation of their wisdom would sink, and that their interest would be much depressed, if they could not run it down: and if all other things failed, then they would fly to this, that such or such things pleased our ancestors, and it were well for us if we could but match them. They would set up their rest on such an answer, as a sufficient confutation of all that could be said: as if it were a great misfortune, that any should be found wiser than his ancestors; but though they willingly let go all the good things that were among those of former ages, yet if better things are proposed they cover themselves obstinately with this excuse of reverence to past times."

There follows an account of the episode at Archbishop Morton's, from which we have already quoted a passage. Then the theme is taken up again, More asserting: "I cannot change my opinion; for I still think that if you could overcome that aversion which you have to the Courts of Princes, you might, by the advice which it is in your power to give, do a great deal of good to mankind; and this is the chief design that every good man ought to propose to himself in living; for your friend Plato thinks that nations will be happy, when either philosophers become kings, or kings become philosophers; it is no wonder if we are so far from that happiness, while philosophers will not think it their duty to assist kings with their councils." "They are not so base-minded," said he, "but that they would willingly do it; many of them have already done it by their books, if those that are in power would but hearken to their good advice. But Plato judged right, that except kings themselves became philosophers, they who from their childhood are corrupted with false notions, would never fall in entirely with the councils of philosophers, and this he himself found to be true in the person of Dionysius.

"Do not you think, that if I were about any king, proposing good laws to him, and endeavouring to root out all the cursed seeds of evil that I found in him, I should either be turned out of his Court, or at least be laughed at for my pains? For instance, what could it signify if I were about the King of France, and were called into his Cabinet Council, where several wise men, in his hearing, were proposing many expedients: as by what arts and practices Milan may be kept; and Naples, that had so oft slipped out of their hands, recovered; how many Venetians, and after them the rest of Italy, may be subdued; and then how Flanders, Brabant and all Burgundy, and some other kingdoms which he had swallowed already in his designs, may be added to his empire. One proposes a league with the Venetians, to be kept as long as he finds his account in it, and that he ought to communicate councils with them, and give them some share of the spoil, till his success make him need or fear them less, and then it will be easily taken out of their hands. Another proposes the hiring the Germans, and the securing the Switzers by pensions. Another proposes the gaining the Emperor by money, which is omnipotent with him. Another proposes a peace with the King of Aragon, and in order to cement it, the yielding up the King of Navarre's pretensions. Another thinks the Prince of Castile is to be wrought on, by the hope of an alliance; and that some of his courtiers are to be gained by the French faction by pensions. The hardest point of all is what to do with England: a treaty of peace is to be set on foot, and if their alliance is not to be depended on, yet it is to be made as firm as possible; and they are to be called friends but suspected as enemies: therefore the Scots are to be kept in readiness, to be let loose upon England on every occasion: and some banished nobleman is to be supported underhand (for by the league it cannot be done avowedly) who has a pretension to the Crown, by which means the suspected prince may be kept in awe. Now when things are in so great a fermentation, and so many gallant men are joining councils, how to carry on the war, if so mean a man as I should stand up and wish them to change all their councils to let Italy alone and stay at home, since the kingdom of France was indeed greater than could be well governed by one man; that therefore he ought not to think of adding others to it: and if after this, I should propose to them the resolutions of the

Achorians, a people that lie on the South East of Utopia, who long ago engaged in war, in order to add to the dominions of their prince another kingdom, to which he had some pretensions by an ancient alliance. This they conquered, but found that the trouble of keeping it was equal to that by which it had been gained; that the conquered people were always either in rebellion or exposed to foreign invasions, while they were obliged to be incessantly at war, either for or against them, and consequently could never disband their army; that in the meantime they were oppressed with taxes, their money went out of the kingdom, their blood was spilt for the glory of their king, without procuring the least advantage to the people, who received not the smallest benefit from it even in time of peace; and that their manners being corrupted by a long war, robbery and murders everywhere abounded, and their laws fell into contempt; while their king, distracted with the care of two kingdoms, was the less able to apply his mind to the interests of either. When he saw this, and that there would be no end to these evils, they by joint councils made a humble address to their king, desiring him to choose which of the two kingdoms he had the greatest mind to keep, since he could not hold both; for they were too great a people to be governed by a divided king, since no man would willingly have a groom that should be in common between him and another. Upon which the good prince was forced to quit his new kingdom to one of his friends (who was not long after dethroned), and to be content with his old one. To this I would add that after all those warlike attempts the vast confusions, and the consumption both of treasure and of people that must follow them; perhaps upon some misfortune they might be forced to throw up all at last; therefore it seemed much more eligible that the king should improve his ancient kingdom all he could, and make it flourish as much as possible; that he should love his people, and be loved by them; that he should live amongst them, govern them gently, and let other kingdoms alone, since that which had fallen to his share was big enough, if not too big for him. Pray how do you think such a speech as this would be heard?" "I confess," said More, "I think not very well."

"But what," said he, "if I should sort with another kind of ministers, whose chief contrivances and consultations were, by what art the prince's treasures might be increased. Where one proposes raising the value of specie when the king's debts are large, and lowering it when his revenues were to come in, that so he might both pay much with a little, and in a little receive a great deal: another proposes a pretence of a war, that money might be raised in order to carry it on, and that a peace be concluded as soon as that was done; and this with such appearances of religion as might work on the people, and make them impute it to the piety of their prince, and to his tenderness for the lives of his subjects; a third revives some old musty laws and proposes the levying the penalties of these laws, that as it would bring in a vast treasure so there might be a good pretence for it, since it would look like the executing of a law, and the doing of justice. A fourth proposes the prohibiting of many things under severe penalties, especially such as were against the interests of the people, and then the dispensing with these prohibitions upon great compositions, to those who might find their advantage in breaking them. This would serve two ends, both of them acceptable to many; for as those whose avarice led them to transgress would be severely fined, so the selling licenses dear would look as if a prince were tender to his people and would not easily or at low rates dispense with anything that might be against the public good. Another proposes that the judges must be made

sure, that they may declare always in favour of the prerogative, that they must be often sent for to Court, that the
king may hear them argue those points in which he is
concerned; since how unjust soever any of his pretensions
may be, yet still some one or other of them, either out of
contradiction to others or the pride of singularity, or to
make their court, would out some pretence or other to
give the king a fair colour to carry the point: for if the
judges but differ in the opinion, the clearest thing in the
world is made by that means disputable, and truth being
once brought in question, the king may then take advantage to expound the law for his own profit, while the
judges that stand out will be brought over, either out of
fear or modesty, and they being thus gained, all of them
may be sent to the bench to give sentence boldly, as the
king would have it: for fair pretence will never be wanting
when sentence is to be given in the prince's favour.   It
will either be said that equity lies on his side, or some
words in the law will be found sounding that way, or
some forced sense will be put to them: and when all things
fail, the king's undoubted prerogative will be pretended, as
that which is above all law: and to which a religious judge
ought to have a special regard.   Thus all consent to that
maxim of Grassus, that a prince cannot have treasure
enough, since he must maintain his armies out of it: that a
king, even though he would, can do nothing unjustly; that
all property is in him, not excepting the very persons of
his subjects: that no man has any other property, but
that which the king out of his goodness thinks fit to leave
him.   And they think it is the prince's interests that there
be as little of this left as may be, as if it were his advantage
that his people should have neither riches or liberty,
since these things make them less easy and less willing
to submit to a cruel and unjust government; whereas
necessity and poverty blunts them, makes them patient,

beats them down, and breaks that height of spirit, that might otherwise dispose them to rebel.

"What success could I count on with my principles under such councils of the king ?" asks Raphael.

The whole passage is a scorching satire on the contemporary monarchy. It constitutes More's political confession of faith, and his justification for holding aloof from the Court.

5. *More Enters the King's Service.*

Two years after More wrote *Utopia* we find him at Court at the start of his short but brilliant career, which was to lead him in little more than a decade to the highest position in the kingdom below the king, that of Lord Chancellor. What happened during these two years to bring about such a change in More's outlook ?

In our view, the clue to More's transformation is to be sought in the success which *Utopia* met with.

This was enormous, not only in the learned world, but also amongst statesmen. We may very well suppose that *Utopia* heightened More's influence in London itself.

His communism frightened nobody, for no communist party then existed. His criticism of absolutism, his plea that the king should attend to the welfare of his subjects rather than prosecute wars, were demands which openly and boldly expressed the yearnings of the aspiring middle class.

In feudal times the king had been pre-eminently the leader in war, and had never interfered with economic processes.

The modern king, the leader of the bourgeoisie, ought, above all, to facilitate the enrichment of the middle class, not frowning on war itself so much as on every war that was not in the interests of commerce. And as out of mere vanity and under the influence of the feudal tradition Henry had become involved in such wars, More's injunctions found strong support among the middle class.

In the eyes of Humanists and of the middle class More's communism was a high-minded enthusiasm, but his criticism of existing political conditions went right to their hearts.

This explains the great influence of *Utopia* on its contemporaries, an influence which even Henry VIII. could not escape. With his *Utopia* More had sketched a general political programme which won general applause, and this brought him into the front rank of English politicians. Even if he would, he could now no longer hold aloof from Court, precisely because of his bold criticism of the existing absolutism.

More had ceased to be a private individual. The favourite of London, England's predominant city, and the favourite of the Humanists, who created public opinion, he had become a political factor to be won or destroyed. Henry had already tried to win More. Now he strained every effort to attract him to his service. Refusal of overtures so urgently made would have drawn upon him the enmity of the all-powerful king, and was then synonymous with high treason, often involving execution. Absolutism would tolerate a private opposition no more than a public one; it acted on the principle: who is not for me is against me.

While, on the one hand, consequent upon the success of *Utopia*, the pressure on More to overcome his disinclination towards the Court was much stronger than it had previously been, on the other hand, this resolution itself was weakening. We have every reason for thinking that the impression made by *Utopia* was so great that Henry was obliged to make concessions and lighten the burdens of the people.

It is certain that a few months after the appearance of *Utopia* Henry abandoned his war policy and surrendered a portion of his French conquests. In February, 1518, Tournai was given back to France and a marriage was arranged between the Dauphin and Henry's daughter Mary. This marked the close of England's wars with France, a tradition handed down from feudal times.

In 1516 Cardinal Wolsey had become Lord Chancellor. He was a man well disposed towards the Humanists, and Seebohm concludes from various indications that Wolsey admitted that the principles of *Utopia* ought to be enforced at least to the extent of reducing the annual expenditure.

A policy of peace, economy, sympathy with Humanism: these were the prospects then offered by Henry VIII.'s Court. They were illusory, but there they were. Ought More, under these circumstances, to persist in a resistance which might cost him his head ? Ought he not rather to engage in public activity, in spite of his forebodings ? Was there any other chance of doing useful work, from his standpoint, than at the Court of his prince ? Might not Henry VIII. be amenable to rational advice ? And was it not better to make the attempt rather than nurse his anger in inaction and merely to write Utopias ?

Only this line of reasoning, combined with the effects of *Utopia*, in our opinion, render More's change of side intelligible, as otherwise it would remain an enigma, in the case of a character such as his, which held tenaciously to its convictions and had no desire for money or honours.

In fact, we have not found any other explanation attempted, nor was an explanation necessary for people who regarded *Utopia* as a mere literary exercise, such as most of More's biographers.

Seebohm alone has attempted to explain the apparent contradiction between More's political principles and his activities between 1516 and 1518. He finds it in the literary success of *Utopia*, which caused Henry to deem it advisable to win over More, and made the latter hope that his advice would be heeded.

We agree with Seebohm on this point, although the influence which More gained as a writer does not seem to us sufficient to explain why Henry VIII. attached so much importance to securing his services and retaining them. In our opinion, too little regard has hitherto been paid to the fact that More had become the representative of one of the most powerful and enterprising classes in England. Only More's importance for London and London's importance for England provides us with a clue to the influence of *Utopia* and the influence of its author on the English Court.

6. *More's Contest with Lutheranism.*

At the time More came to Henry VIII.'s Court, the Reformation movement which had begun in Germany in the previous year was beginning to spread in England. More was obliged to adopt an attitude towards it; like the overwhelming majority of other Humanists he emphatically opposed the movement as soon as it was clear that it signified the separation of the constituent parts of Christendom from the Papacy, the break-up of Christendom.

We have already discussed the reasons why Humanists in general opposed the Reformation. These reasons had a special influence with More. In a previous chapter we have shown that they were not of an ecclesiastical character. More clearly perceived the abuses of the Church and did not hesitate to reveal them. If despite this the Catholic Church persists in numbering him among her saints, because he abused Luther, she can give him good company. She can, for example, put by his side Rabelais, who would also have nothing to do with the Reformation, and empties the vials of his mockery upon Calvin.

The motives which led More to oppose the Reformation are to be sought in the political and economic sphere. When the author of the present treatise began to study More's writings he was of the opinion that More's hostility to the Reformation, so far as it partook of a political nature, was to be ascribed to his hostility to absolutism. This opinion has proved to be untenable. As we have seen, More was no opponent of monarchy, which, on the contrary, he held to be extremely necessary, like the great majority of Humanists. Scarcely any class in the sixteenth century regarded the monarchy as more necessary than did the merchants. Now More was in a practical respect the representative of their class interests, although in his theoretical outlook he was more advanced. Capital has always called for " order," only occasionally for " freedom." Order was its most important vital element; More, who had become great in the minds of the London middle class, was therefore a " man of order " who disliked nothing more than independent action of the people. All for the people, but nothing by the people, was his watchword.

The German Reformation, however, was in its inception a popular movement. The common exploiter of all classes of the German nation was the Roman Papacy. When once a class rose against the latter, it necessarily drew the other classes with it. Cities, knights, peasants, all rebelled against Rome with a tumult that almost frightened the princes. Only as the movement progressed did the struggle against the Romish exploitation among the lower classes become a struggle against exploitation in general, and the national rebellion of Germany against Rome a civil war, a peasants' war. And only since the strength of the lower classes was broken in this internal strife has the Reformation in Germany tended to assume the shape of a purely dynastic affair.

At the outset the Lutherans addressed themselves to all classes of the nation; only when they saw that the antagonisms within the nation were irreconcilable and that they had to come down on the side of a definite class, did they elect to support princedom.

This transformation of Lutheranism was not manifest until after the great peasant war of 1525. We can therefore understand why More came to attack the Lutheran doctrines on account of their danger to monarchy. He did this in 1523 in a Latin treatise: *Thomas More's Answer to the Insults which Martin Luther has heaped on Henry VIII.*

The title tells us what caused the polemic. We have already mentioned Henry VIII.'s book against Luther respecting the "Seven Sacraments." This book was answered by Luther, not in the politest fashion, in the following year.

More rejoined in his above-mentioned treatise with equal bluntness in the Latin language. Atterbury opined that of all the men of his time More possessed the greatest facility of abuse in good Latin. The personal attacks on Luther, who is held up as drunkard and ignorant, fill the greatest part of the *Answer*. It contains, however, a defence of the Papacy and an indication of the political danger of the new doctrines. Thus it is stated, among other things: "The enemies of the Christian faith have every time proved to be enemies of the Holy Stool. If, however, the office is to be blamed for the faults of men, as the Lutherans calumniate the Papacy in the most dastardly manner, it is not the Papacy alone, but also the Monarchy, and all political chiefs generally that are assailed and the people will find themselves disorderly and lawless. And yet it is better for the community to have bad guides than none at all. It is, therefore, wiser to reform the Papacy than to abolish it."

Five years later More published his *Dialogue Concerning Heresies and Matters of Religion*. In this he enters rather more upon theological discussions, but the most important are those of a secular character. The following passage seems to us particularly illuminating for More's attitude towards the Reformation: "And one special thing with which he (Luther) spiced all the poison was the liberty that he so highly commended unto the people, bringing them in belief that having faith they needed nothing else. For as for fasting, prayer, and such other things, he taught them to neglect and set at naught as vain and unfruitful ceremonies, teaching them also that being faithful Christians, so were us near cousins to Christ that they be in a full freedom and liberty discharged of all governors and all manner of laws spiritual or temporal except the gospel only. And albeit he said that of a special perfection it should be well done to suffer the rule and authority of popes, princes, and other governors, which rule and authority he called but only tyranny, yet he saith that the people be so free by faith that they be no more bounden thereto than they be bound to suffer wrong. And this doctrine also teacheth Tyndall as the special matter of his Whole Book of Disobedience. Now was this doctrine in Germany of the common uplandish people so pleasantly harsh, that it blinded them in the looking upon the remainder and could not suffer them to consider and see what end the same would in conclusion come to. The temporal lords were glad also to hear this gibe against the clergy and the people as glad to hear it against the clergy and against the lords too, and against all other governors of every good town and city, and finally, so far went it forward that at the last it began to burst out and

10

fall to open force and violence. For intending to begin at the feeblest there gathered them together for the letting forth of these ungracious heresies a boisterous company of the unhappy sect, and first rebelled against an abbot and after against a bishop, wherewith the temporal lords had good game sport and dissembled the matter, gaping after the lands of the spirituality till they had almost played as Æsop telleth of the dog which to snatch at the shadow of the cheese in the water let fall and lost the cheese that he bear in his mouth. For so was it shortly after that those uplandish Lutherans took so great boldness and so began to grow strong that they set also upon the temporal lords. Which had they not set hand thereto the sooner while they looked for other men's lands, had been like shortly to lose their own. But so quit they themself that they flew upon the point of 70,000 Lutherans in one summer and subdued the remnant in that part of Germany to a right miserable servitude. Howbeit meanwhile many mischievous deeds they did, and yet in divers other parts of Germany and Switzerland this ungracious sect by the negligence of the governors in great cities is so seriously grown that finally the common people have compelled the rulers to follow them, who if they had taken heed in time they might have ruled and led."

Here we find the class struggle which underlay the Reformation to a certain extent distinctly portrayed by a contemporary of the Reformation, although More did not see that the struggle against the Papacy was a struggle against exploitation.

This was due to the peculiar economic position of England, of which we shall speak in the next part. Here we are only concerned to show that one of the political reasons which caused More to oppose the Reformation was its popular character, its character as a national, as a popular movement. But its national character was distasteful to him in another sense. Like many other Humanists, More had a strong national and a strong international bias at the same time. In Italy, the native country of Humanism, this seemingly contradictory attitude was determined by the economic conditions. As we have shown, the unity of the whole of Christendom under the Papacy was in Italy's national interest, or rather in the material interest of Italy's ruling class. Outside Italy, and particularly in the non-Romance countries, this international sentiment had no material support, and was a mere ideological whim, without any influence on the people. In any case More's internationalism seems to find an explanation in the actual conditions. More was, as we know, an opponent of dynastic wars, and therefore a representative of real material interests, which required that union and peace should prevail in Christendom; it was, however, an illusion to believe that Catholicism was still capable of representing this unifying force. The Pope himself had become a secular prince, competing with his colleagues in diplomatic intrigues and dynastic wars.

7. *More in Conflict with the Monarchy.*

Common hostility to Lutheranism was bound to bring Henry VIII. and More closer together. Meanwhile More's business knowledge and importance grew. No wonder he advanced rapidly. Appointments as Master of Requests and Privy Councillor followed in quick succession; within a few years Henry appointed him Treasurer of the Exchequer and shortly afterwards Chancellor of the Duchy of Lancaster, which post he held until 1529. His elevation to the knighthood would fall within this time.

But More no more allowed himself to be bribed by these

posts of honour than he was led into unconditional subjection to the monarchy by his antagonism to popular movements.   That he was independent towards the monarchy, and that neither Court service nor the Reformation had altered his attitude, that the rule of the king, as the shepherd of his people, was necessary, while subjection to tyrants, to shearers of the people, was shameful, was proved when Wolsey caused him to be elected as Speaker of Parliament in 1523.

This Parliament had, of course, as its chief task, to grant money.   More's task there was no pleasant one; the Speaker functioned not merely as president of the proceedings of the Lower House, but he had also to compile the budget and present it to the House, and therefore performed some of the functions of the modern Chancellor of the Exchequer.

Henry, of course, thought it was More's business to make his demands plausible to the Commons; and this was in any event necessary, for the Lower House was by no means disposed to grant new taxes.   Cardinal and Lord Chancellor Wolsey, much irritated, went himself to intimidate Parliament, in which task he counted on More's assistance.

As Roper tells us, he perceived with angry surprise that the man he had chosen to be his tool defended the rights of the Lower House against the all-powerful minister. Beside himself with rage, he rushed out of Parliament. Eventually Henry achieved his object, but only after he had intimidated Parliament with threats.

Serious objections have been raised to this account of Roper's and the matter has not yet been cleared up. We must leave it at that, and likewise Roper's statements that it was desired to get rid of the inconvenient man, but that he could not be openly attacked, as he had gained rather than lost influence with the citizens by his courageous championship of the rights of the Lower House.   It was therefore sought, under the appearance of a promotion, to procure his removal from the country by sending him as Ambassador to Spain. More perceived the trap and refused the honour which Henry offered him " on the grounds of health."

However that may be, More was soon to come into serious conflict with the King, which finally ended with a promotion of another kind.

Henry VIII. was married to Catherine of Spain, the widow of his brother Arthur. This lady, however, became the more tedious to him the older she grew, and when he became acquainted with Anne Boleyn, one of his Court ladies, a pretty and witty girl who had learnt and practised all the arts of coquetry at the French Court, he fell so violently in love as to conceive the project of marrying Anne and divorcing Catherine. As the Pope would not grant the divorce, Henry broke away from the Catholic Church and started the Reformation in England.

Such are the circumstances which make world history, as they are usually narrated, and in this instance they almost compel belief.

According to this account, England would still be Catholic to-day if Henry had been less amorous and Anne less coquettish.

In reality the grounds and even the occasion of the separation of the Church lay somewhat deeper than a mere amour. Many Catholic princes had unattractive wives, and attractive mistresses as well, before and after Henry VIII. without a separation of the Catholic Church arising therefrom; and many Popes before and after Henry VIII. pronounced divorces when they thought fit. We have therefore to enquire whence it came that Henry's divorce gave the impulse to such an extensive transformation.

The marriages of absolute monarchs, especially in the

sixteenth century, had a peculiar character. The realms
of absolute princes were their domains, over which they
exercised complete control, and which they strove to
augment as much as possible. States had not yet attained
the consistency of modern national States, and were still
in a state of constant flux; here a fragment was detached
and there a fragment was added; here two countries were
united by marriage; there territory was rounded off with
a small neighbour by the treaty of inheritance. Among
the princes as among the great landowners there was a
frenzied greed for land, and consequently everlasting wars,
diplomatic intrigues, and alliances which were broken as
easily as they were concluded. The strongest diplomatic
alliance was that sealed by an alliance of marriage, which
enabled spies and agents to be placed by the side of the
friend at Court in the shape of the spouse. While excessive
confidence would not be placed on the marriage alliance,
it offered a better guarantee than a mere piece of parch-
ment, and the inheritance claims which arose from the
marriage might, in certain circumstances, be extremely
useful.

It may be imagined in what light the " sanctity of
marriage" appeared under these circumstances. Children
were paired with each other; old women with boys, old
men with schoolgirls.

Thus, as we have said, England's attachment to Spain
under Henry VII. was strengthened by the marriage of
Catherine of Aragon with Henry's eldest son Arthur.
At the time of his betrothal Arthur was six years old.
When eleven years old he married, and he died the following year. Seven years later Arthur's widow married his
younger brother, afterwards Henry VIII.

The marriage had been delayed because Henry did not
wholly trust his father-in-law, who did not want to pay
the promised dowry.

In the course of Henry's reign a change came over the relations between England and Spain. By uniting in his hands Spain, the Netherlands, and, the German Imperial Crown, Charles V. had become a formidable power, completely overshadowing France, and rendering superfluous the Anglo-Spanish Alliance which had been directed against the preponderance of France. England's friendship with Spain suffered an eclipse, and was replaced by an alliance with France. Thus the marriage with Catherine had become purposeless. The divorce was promoted not alone by Henry, but by his minister Cardinal Wolsey, who, however, wanted not Anne but a French princess to take Catherine's place.

The same motives which impelled Henry and Wolsey to promote the divorce, impelled the Pope to oppose it. At the precise time when the divorce affair assumed its acutest form, from 1527 to 1533, the Pope was most completely dependent on Charles V., who was Catherine's nephew. Clement VII. made every effort to satisfy Henry; he would even have granted him the divorce (and he would have been a poor Pope not to have found a canonical reason therefor), but Charles would not hear of such a concession.

He so accentuated the dispute as to leave the Pope the choice of being England's tool or Spain's.

The Lutherans explained they could not assent to the divorce, but they advised Henry to follow the example of Abraham and Jacob and take two wives. Luther even permitted the Landgrave of Hesse to live in bigamy, "on account of the drunkenness and ugliness of the Landgravine."

Henry contemptuously rejected the Lutheran permission. He imagined in his pride that he could compete with the powers which then strove for the domination and exploitation of the Papacy, with Francis I. of France and the Spanish-German Hapsburg, Charles. He even aspired to the German Imperial Crown. And when Pope Leo X. died, Wolsey applied for the tiara, as he also did on the death of Leo's successor. On both occasions Henry was forced to suffer the humiliation of seeing creatures of Charles chosen instead of his own creatures—*viz.*, Hadrian VI. (1522 to 1523) and Clement VII. The affair of the divorce completely convinced Henry that it was useless to attempt to dominate the Papacy, and therefore, if he was not to be under the heel of the Papacy, if he wanted to be master of the country and master of the Church, there was no alternative but separation from Rome.

To this political motive was added an economic motive: the great treasure which the miserly Henry VII. had bequeathed had long been dissipated in war and luxury. The Parliament of 1523 had shown that however pliable it might be in other respects, it was not to be relied on for large money grants. What lay nearer to hand than to imitate what had been done so well by the cousins in Germany, to end financial embarrassment by the confiscation of Church property. Although the dissolution of the monasteries was not proceeded with until after More's death, it was already threatened in his lifetime, thus intimidating the priesthood and impelling it to purchase the despot's favour by large grants of money. The confiscation of property was not resorted to until nothing considerable remained to be extorted.

In no other country was the separation of the Church so flagrant, so shameless, such a mere result of the lust, arrogance, and greed of absolutism as in England. No change was made in the dogmas and the ritual except that the King took the place of the Pope. Lutheranism was forbidden equally with popery.

It is clear that, with his international outlook, More

could no more sympathise with this kind of Reformation than with the beginnings of Lutheranism. He was constrained to oppose the foundation of any national Church. Nor could he assent to any augmentation of the princely power. On the contrary, he desired to restrict it, at least, not so much from below as from above. He felt the necessity of a limitation, a subordination of absolutism; he did not, however, think that the requisite force for this was to be found in the people, and therefore took refuge in a doctrinal illusion, which he shared with many Humanists, and which we have already touched on in the first part: that the prince ought to be guided by the Pope, above whom should stand the council, the latter being inspired with the spirit of Humanism. The old bottles should remain, the wine should be renewed. And then the monarchy desired to transform the Church from a brake into a tool! In this More could not assist.

He had long kept to himself his objections to Henry's Reformation. It was not until after he had been pronounced guilty at his trial that he spoke out and declared that England, which only formed a small part of the whole of Christendom, could no more make laws which contradicted the general laws of the Church than the City of London could legislate against an Act of Parliament. And he added:

" I nothing doubt but that, though not in this Realm, yet in Christendom about, of these well learned bishops and virtuous men that are yet alive, they be not the fewer part that are of my mind therein. Therefore, I am not bounden to conform my conscience to the council of one realm, against the general council of all Christendom."

This is a plain enough utterance in the language of his time.

More's standpoint was as bold as it was untenable.

We have already drawn attention to the instability of German and English Humanism, to which we have attributed its rapid disappearance. The majority of Humanists were mere theorists, professors, and men of letters, who withdrew into the background when the storm of the Reformation burst. A fiery spirit like More would not do this, nor could he have done so had he wished. His political influence was too great for him to be allowed to vanish unregarded. He must either serve the king or perish. In view of his character, these alternatives sealed his fate.

But it was some time before Nemesis overtook him. It was already preparing as More was in the ascendant, and was promoted to the highest position in the realm below the king. At any rate, from the start he had opposed the divorce. Henry hoped, however, up to the last minute to win him over, and he had every reason to continue his efforts, as More's popularity was then greater than ever.

In 1529, More, together with Cuthbert Tunstall and John Haclet, was sent to Cambrai, to represent England in the peace negotiations between England and France on the one side and Spain on the other side. The peace was specially important for the English merchants, as the trade with the Netherlands had suffered considerably from the war. More and his companions conducted the negotiations with great skill, and secured a treaty favourable beyond all expectations with which the English, and particularly the merchants, were extremely pleased.

Such a useful and popular man had to be won over, if this was at all possible.

When, therefore, Wolsey succumbed to the intrigues of Anne Boleyn, More was appointed Lord Chancellor in his place, being the first layman not a member of the higher nobility to occupy this post. He accepted the position reluctantly, but he had no choice. His frame of mind may be gleaned from his installation speech.

The Dukes of Norfolk and Suffolk led him in public procession through Westminster Hall, where More assumed his position before the assembled people. The Duke of Norfolk made a flattering speech, praising the merits of the new Lord Chancellor, to which More replied that he was not so delighted at his promotion as other people thought, when he remembered his wise and powerful predecessor and the latter's fall.

" I ascend this seat as a post full of troubles and dangers and without any real honour. The higher the post of honour the greater the fall, as the example of my predecessor proves."

His gloomy forebodings were destined soon to be fulfilled. He tried to remain neutral, but in vain. He was soon confronted with the request to put his name to actions which he profoundly disapproved of. Henry compelled him to read to the Lower House the opinions of the Universities of Paris, Orleans, Angers, Bruges, Toulouse, Bologna, and Padua, which he had bought, and those of Oxford and Cambridge, which had been extorted: these opinions declared Henry's divorce to be canonically valid. Then More perceived that to remain in office any longer was incompatible with his convictions, and he resigned his position in 1532.

8. *More's Downfall.*

With his retirement More's fate was decided. He had declared against the tyrant at a moment when the latter needed all his servants and had embarked on a struggle against bodies of citizens of his own realm. To retire in such circumstances was, in the eyes of the King, to favour rebellion and high treason.

More withdrew completely from public life without deceiving himself for a moment as to what awaited him. But the blow was longer in coming than he thought. More's influence and reputation were too great for Henry to neglect any means of winning him before he destroyed him. Rewards and honours proved unavailing. Perhaps he might be moved by threats and coerced by necessity.

A system of chicanery and torments began. More's property, which was not very considerable, was confiscated by the king. More did not possess much cash, being poorer at the close of his Court career than at the commencement. He now lived at Chelsea in great need.

In 1533 a charge of high treason was brought against a Canterbury nun, Elizabeth Barton, called the Maid of Kent, an impostor who pretended to see visions. She had prophesied that the king would not live a month after his marriage with Anne Boleyn. More was drawn into the trial because he had once chanced to meet the nun; he had adopted a very reserved attitude, recognising at once that she was an impostor. The charge was so unfounded and More's reputation so great that the Lords refused to pass the Bill which declared the nun of Kent and her coadjutors guilty of high treason, unless More's name was struck out of it. To this Henry was obliged to assent. The nun, together with six others, was executed. More came through this unscathed.

The Duke of Norfolk pressed him to submit to the King. "It is dangerous to strive with princes, and I would rather that you fell in with the king's wishes, for by God a prince's anger means death." "Is that all, my Lord?" replied More. "That makes only this difference between you and I, that I die to-day and you to-morrow."

In November, 1533, Parliament passed the Act of Supremacy, which made the King the supreme head of the English Church. Moreover, Parliament ordained that

Henry's first marriage was invalid and his second lawful: it excluded Catherine's daughter Mary from the succession and declared Anne's daughter Elizabeth to be Henry's lawful successor. An oath was drawn up embodying the recognition of this principle and submitted to all the priests in London and Westminster, and, in addition, to More. He refused to swear the entire oath, but declared his willingness to subscribe to the part that referred to the succession. In consequence of this refusal he was arrested and imprisoned in the Tower. There he remained for more than a year, poorly nourished, and soon deprived of his books as well: in vain; physically he could be broke, but not morally; he persisted in his refusal to take the oath.

Finally he was brought to trial.

Parliament had prescribed no punishment for refusing to take the oath. To remedy this defect, it was later declared to be high treason for anybody maliciously to attempt to deprive the King of his title as head of the English Church.

More had maintained an obstinate silence respecting his reasons for refusing the oath, but silence is not high treason. In their embarrassment the authorities made use of a peculiar witness, the Attorney-General, Rich, who asserted that More had confided to him that Parliament had no right to make the king head of the Church.

In vain More pointed out how absurd it was to suppose he would make a confession to a man whom he had long held as of no credit which he had made to nobody else. In vain other witnesses who were present at Rich's interview with More in the town declared that they had heard nothing. The jury were worthy of the witness. They found More guilty without more ado. He was sentenced to be hanged: drawn, mutilated, and quartered.

The King allowed More to be beheaded, at which he

exclaimed, "God preserve my friends from such favour." His humour did not desert More, and his last words were a jest.

On July 6 he was executed in the Tower. The scaffold was badly put together, and it swayed as he ascended it. He therefore remarked to the lieutenant of the Tower who conducted him: "Pray you see me safe up, and for my coming down let me shift for myself." Then he tried to speak to the people, but was prevented from doing so. "And after he prayed he turned to the executioner," relates Roper, "and with a cheerful countenance spake thus unto him: 'Pluck up thy spirits, man, and be not afraid to do thine office. My neck is very short; take heed thou strike not awry.'"

Thus died the first of the great communist Utopians.

PART III
UTOPIA

CHAPTER I

MORE AS ECONOMIST AND SOCIALIST

1. *The Roots of More's Socialism.*

As a Humanist and a politician, More was in the front rank of his contemporaries, as a Socialist he was far ahead of them all. His political, religious, and Humanist writings are to-day only read by a small number of historians. Had he not written *Utopia* his name would scarcely be better known to-day than that of the friend who shared his fate, Bishop Fisher of Rochester. His socialism made him immortal.

Whence originated this socialism ?

Unlike the historians of the idealistic school, we do not believe in a Holy Spirit which illumines minds and fills them with ideas, to which the political and economic development adapts itself. We rather start from the assumption that the contradictions and antagonisms which the economic development creates in society stimulate thought and provoke investigations by men who are favourably situated to prosecute such researches, so that they may understand what is going on before their eyes and remove the suffering which contemporary conditions entail. In this way arise political and social ideas which influence contemporary thought, or at least, particular

159

classes, in the degree that they respond to the actual
conditions, and which are correct so far as they coincide
with the interests of the aspiring classes.

So it comes about that certain ideas are only operative
under certain conditions, that ideas which at one time
encounter indifference and even scorn are taken up with
enthusiasm, and often without strict verification, a few
decades later.   Idealist historians are unable to explain
why this is so; they are therefore obliged in the last resort
to seek refuge in God, in a mystery, like all idealist philosophers; it is the " time spirit " which decides whether or
not an idea shall achieve social validity.

The materialist conception of history alone explains
the influence of particular ideas.   It is not concerned to
deny that every age has its particular ideas which condition it, and that these ideas form the dynamics of social
development.   It does not, however, stop at this point,
but proceeds to investigate the forces which set the
machinery in motion, and these it finds in the material
conditions.

It is clear that ideas must be fermenting for some
time before they can exercise any influence on the
masses.   There is a tendency to reproach the masses
with running after novelties, whereas the truth is that
they cling most obstinately to the old.   The antagonism of the new economic conditions to the transmitted
conditions and the ideas which accord therewith must
be fairly pronounced before it penetrates to the mind
of the masses.   Where the acumen of the investigator
perceives unbridgable antagonisms of classes, the average man sees only accidental personal disputes; where
the investigator sees social evils which could only
be removed by social transformations, the average man
consoles himself with the hope that times are only temporarily bad and will soon improve.   We are not speaking

of the members of classes on the decline, most of whom will not face facts, but have in mind the nascent classes, whose interests it is to see, but who cannot see until they bump right up against the new conditions. Their ideas also were conditioned by the newly developing material conditions, but these conditions were not yet sharply defined enough to render the aspiring classes accessible to these ideas.

But a thinker who takes his stand on the material conditions may be a whole epoch in advance of his time, if he perceives a newly evolving mode of production and its social consequences not only sooner than most of his contemporaries, but straining far into the future, also glimpses the more rational mode of production into which it will develop.

Thomas More is one of the few who have been capable of this bold intellectual leap; at a time when the capitalist mode of production was in its infancy, he mastered its essential features so thoroughly that the alternative mode of production which he elaborated and contrasted with it as a remedy for its evils, contained several of the most important ingredients of Modern Socialism. The drift of his speculations, of course, escaped his contemporaries, and can only be properly appreciated by us to-day. Despite the immense economic and technical transformations of the last three hundred years, we find in *Utopia* a number of tendencies which are still operative in the Socialist Movement of our time.

Our first enquiry pertains to the causes of such an extraordinary phenomenon. If we are not to resort to spiritism and clairvoyance, there must have been a peculiar chain of circumstances which inclined More alone in his age towards socialist theories—Münzer's socialism was of a character quite different from More's, and cannot therefore be taken into account.

11

Despite the fact that, for obvious reasons, none of More's biographers has dealt with this question and that More himself gives us but few hints, we think we are able to indicate at least some of these causes, partly personal, partly of a local nature, which in conjunction with the general situation as we have sketched it in the first part, explain why Socialism found a theoretical expression earlier than Capitalism.

These circumstances are, put shortly, More's personal character, his philosophical training, his activity in practical affairs, and the economic situation of England.

More's personal character may indeed be regarded as one of the causes of his Socialism. Erasmus tells us how amiable, helpful, and full of sympathy with the poor and oppressed More was: he called him the protector of all the poor.

Only in the northern countries of Western Europe were the material conditions in the sixteenth century favourable to the formation of such a disinterested character. In the mercantile republics of Italy, as in the Courts of the Romance monarchies, egotism, the grand feature of the new mode of production, reigned absolutely; it reigned openly, boldly, full of revolutionary defiance. It was a vast egotism, quite different from the cowardly, mendacious, despicable egotism of to-day, which hides itself behind conventional hypocrisy.

Generally speaking, in the towns of England and Germany, entirely different economic conditions prevailed from those in the Italian towns, and to a lesser degree in the towns of France and Spain. Agriculture, together with the Mark constitution, still formed to a great extent the basis even of the urban mode of production; the separation of the country from the town was nowhere completely defined.

" As late as the year 1589, the Duke of Bavaria recognised that the burghers of Munich could not exist without commons. Tillage of the soil must then have been a chief support of the citizens '' (L. L. v. Maurer).

At the commencement of the sixteenth century the primitive agrarian communism still existed in England. It had survived under cover of feudalism, and only then began to yield place to another system of agriculture. The features which corresponded to primitive communism still existed, especially among the lower population, and we meet them in More only slightly glossed over with the Humanistic and courtier traits and the self-censure which the conditions imposed upon him. In his serenity, tenacity, unyieldingness, selflessness, and helpfulness we see the impress of all the characteristics of communistic " Merry England."

But sympathy with the poor does not make one a socialist, although without that sympathy no one is likely to become a socialist. In order that socialist sentiments and ideas should grow out of this interest, it must be conjoined with a special economic situation, the existence of a working proletariat as a permanent mass phenomenon, and on the other hand profound economic insight.

The existence of a proletariat of vagabonds creates benevolence and induces almsgiving, but does not produce a socialism of the modern variety.

Now in More's time England was much favoured with respect to the economic development, much more so than, for example, Germany. In respect of the opportunity to appreciate it More's position was almost unique in the northern countries. The only persons who had then learnt to think scientifically and methodically, to generalise, and who were, therefore, capable of formulating a theoretical socialism, were the Humanists. Now in the northern countries Humanism was an exotic growth, in which no class had a special interest. While the

Humanists in Italy were busily engaged in active affairs, and therefore gave expression to the economic and political tendencies of their time and country, the great majority of German Humanists were merely schoolmasters with no glimmering of practical affairs, who, instead of delving into the past for weapons in the struggles of the present, stood aloof from those struggles and retired to their studies, in order to live wholly in the past.

Germany's development did not tend to close the gap between science and life. On the contrary, the rudeness, the barbarism, the boorishness into which Germany sank to an increasing extent after the sixteenth century, and from which she did not emerge until the beginning of the eighteenth century, rendered the maintenance of science in Germany possible only by its being completely divorced from active life.

The fundamental cause of Germany's decay resided in the alteration of the trade routes after the end of the fifteenth century, which not only impeded the economic development in Germany, but transformed it for some time into economic retrogression.

The discoveries of the Portuguese in the second half of the fifteenth century opened a sea route to India. At the same time the old communications with the East through Asia Minor and Egypt were interrupted by the invasions of the Turks, while the caravan routes from Central Asia had previously been closed in consequence of local upheavals.

This paralysed not only the trade of the Mediterranean seaboard, but also that of the towns on the great German waterways, which, besides being the intermediaries of the trade between Italy and the North, traded with the East on their own account by other routes—via Trapezunt and the Black Sea as well as the land route over Russia. The total effect of these changes was to sever the arteries of the German towns, especially of the Hansa towns on the Baltic and the towns in Southern Germany, Nuremberg, Augsburg, etc.

The towns on the Rhine and on the estuaries of the North Sea suffered less, but the trade which they supported was insignificant and its direction had changed. It flowed not from East to West, from South to North, but contrariwise.

Antwerp became for the sixteenth century what Constantinople had been in the fourteenth century and what London was to become in the eighteenth century: the centre of world trade, the focus of the treasures of the East, to which the Americas were now added, whence they were poured out over the whole of Europe.

The proximity of Antwerp inevitably exercised the most stimulating effect upon the commerce of England, and especially of London. And even in More's time England strove to acquire overseas possessions, although as yet without any great success. England's commerce increased as Germany's declined.

Out of mercantile the beginnings of industrial capital were already beginning to develop. Englishmen began to manufacture wool in their own country after the Flemish example, and even in the time of Henry VIII. complaints were heard of the decay of independent handicraft in wool-combing. In Richard III.'s time, Italian merchants in England were accused (An Act touching the merchants of Italy) of buying up large quantities of wool and employing the weavers to prepare it.

But in the England of More the beginnings of the capitalist mode of production in agriculture were much more perceptible than these nuclei of industrial capital. It is one of England's most remarkable peculiarities that capitalism developed there earlier in agriculture than in industry.

The causes of this have already been indicated: they are to be traced to the quality of English wool, which made it a much-sought-after raw material for woollen manufactures.

Next to wool, timber and fuel were important agricultural products in England, in view of the growth of the towns, as was also barley for the Flemish breweries. The demand for wool grew in the degree that manufactures on the one hand, and the means of transport on the other, developed. At the outset English wool found its chief market in the Netherlands, but at the end of the fifteenth century it was being exported both to Italy and to Sweden. Among other things, this may be inferred from two commercial treaties which Henry VII. concluded with Denmark and Florence in 1490.

As the market grew, the merchants and great landowners of England redoubled their efforts to extend wool production. The landowners found the simplest way of doing this was to claim for themselves the common lands which the peasants had a right to use. Thus the peasant was more and more deprived of the opportunity of keeping cattle, his entire business fell into disorder, and financial ruin overtook him. Then the great landowner's land hunger grew more quickly than the peasant was " freed " from the soil. All kinds of expedients were adopted. Not merely individual peasants, but sometimes the inhabitants of entire villages and even small townships were expelled, to make room for sheep.

So long as the landlords themselves farmed their estates, or, as happened for a short period, leased portions of them to tenants, to whom they advanced the necessary agricultural plant, cattle, etc., the expansion of their property was always limited by the plant and stock which the landlord possessed. There was no point in extending his property unless he was able at the same time to add to his plant and stock. This limit melted away and the land hunger of the great landowners knew no bounds with the arrival of the capitalist farmer, who used his own capital to employ wage workers to cultivate the land which he leased. This class arose in England in the last third of the fifteenth century. It rapidly increased in the sixteenth century, in consequence of the unexampled profits which it then made, and which not only accelerated the accumulation of capital, but also attracted capitalists from the towns.

The rise of profits is to be especially attributed to the depreciation of gold and silver which was caused by the immense transfers of the precious metals from America to Europe; the effect of this monetary depreciation may well have been accentuated by the currency debasement of princes.

In the course of the sixteenth century the prices of agricultural products rose by 200 to 300 per cent. in consequence of the currency depreciation. Rents, on the other hand, were slow in rising, as the leases ran for long terms, and did not keep pace with the prices of agricultural products. Therefore they fell actually if not nominally.

The farmers' profits grew at the expense of rents.

This not only increased the number of farmers and the amount of their capital, but also formed a fresh incentive for the large landowners to extend their estates, in order to make good their losses in this way.

The consequence was a rapid impoverishment of the small peasants. A concurrent phenomenon was the dispersal of the feudal bands of retainers, to which we have made reference in the first part.

The retainers were in any case a burden for the working people. Where they remained in existence, they were a burden on the peasants who were obliged to support them. Where they were broken up, they became a scourge to the wage earners, by swelling the ranks of the unemployed.

The fourteenth and fifteenth centuries were the Golden Age for the peasants and wage workers of England.

At the end of this epoch they were both suddenly plunged into deepest poverty. The number of workless swelled to terrible dimensions. The most gruesome punishments were not, of course, calculated either to diminish their numbers or to restrain them from crime: punishment for crime was uncertain, but sure was the punishment for abstention from crime: starvation.

Not much better than the situation of the workless was that of the propertyless workers, who then began to form a numerous class in agriculture. What parliamentary legislation had only incompletely achieved in the preceding two centuries was easily attained in the sixteenth century by the oppressive weight of the reserve army of the workless. Real wages diminished, and labour time was extended.

Food prices rose by 300 per cent., wages only by 150 per cent. From More's time onwards began that steady decay of the English workers in town and country, whose position reached its lowest level in the last quarter of the eighteenth and the first quarter of the nineteenth century, after which it improved, at least for certain sections, owing to trade union organisation.

Wages fell along with rents, profits grew, and so did capitalism.

When capitalism first invades industry and then turns to agriculture, it seems at the outset to wear a benevolent aspect. It must aim at a constant extending of the market, of production, while the importation of labour-power proceeds but slowly. In its early stages, such an industry is always complaining of the lack of labour-power. Capitalists must outbid handicraftsmen and peasants in order to entice away from them their journeymen and bondsmen : wages rise.

In this way capitalism began in many countries; it was hailed as a blessing. Not so in England, where it first invaded and revolutionised agriculture. Improvements in methods of cultivation made many workers superfluous. Capitalism in agriculture meant the direct setting-free of workers. In England this process of setting-free proceeded in its severest forms, at a time when industry was developing but slowly and required only small supplies of labour-power; least of all, the ignorant country labourer.

And hand in hand with the separation of the workers from the land, from their means of production, a rapid concentration of landed property into a few hands was going on.

Nowhere else in Europe, therefore, were the unfavourable reactions of the capitalist mode of production upon the working classes so immediately obvious as in England; nowhere did the unhappy workers clamour so urgently for assistance.

That such an economic situation should cause a man of More's character to reflect and to cast about for means of alleviating the intolerable conditions is what we should expect.

More was not the only person who sought for and propounded such expedients. From numerous writings of that time, from numerous Acts of Parliament we may perceive how deep was the impression made by the economic revolution then proceeding, and how generally the shabby practices of the landlords and their tenants were condemned.

But none of those who put forward remedies had a wider outlook, to none of them came the conviction that the sufferings incident to the new mode of production could only be ended by a transition to another and higher mode of production; none of them, save More, was a Socialist.

A theory of Socialism could only arise within the realm of Humanism. As a Humanist, More learned to think methodically and to generalise. As a Humanist he was enabled to look beyond the horizon of his time and his country: in the writings of classical antiquity he became acquainted with social conditions different from those of his own time. Plato's ideal of an aristocratic communist community must have prompted him to imagine social conditions which, being the opposite of those existing, were free from their concomitant poverty. Plato's authority must have encouraged him to regard such a community as more than a mere figment of the imagination, and to set it up as a goal which humanity should strive to attain.

In so far was Humanism favourable to More's development. But the situation in England was, in a scientific respect, similar to that in Germany: English Humanism remained an imported, exotic growth, without roots in the national life, a mere academic affair. Had More been a mere Humanist, he would hardly have attained to Socialism. We know, however, that More's father, much to the regret of Erasmus and his other Humanist friends, soon tore him away from his studies, in order to put him to the study of law and then to launch him on a practical career. We know in what close relationship More stood to the London merchants, how he was entrusted with the care of their interests on every important occasion. The majority of the positions which More filled impelled him to deal with economic questions; the fact that he was appointed to these posts also proves that he was regarded as an expert in economic matters.

We know that he was a popular advocate, that in 1509 he was appointed Under-Sheriff, in which position he had sufficient opportunity to gain an insight into the economic life of the people. We have also mentioned several missions of which he was a member, for the conduct of commercial negotiations. The first was to Bruges in 1515. In the same year Parliament appointed him a Commissioner of Sewers. His second mission was to Calais in 1517, in order to compose disputes between English and French merchants. In 1520 we find him on a mission to Bruges, to settle disputes between English merchants and the Hansa. Then he became Treasurer, and, in 1523, Speaker in the Commons, both positions presupposing experience in financial matters, and shortly afterwards Chancellor of the Duchy of Lancaster: truly, if anybody had an opportunity to become acquainted with the economic life of his time, it was More. And he became acquainted with it from the most modern standpoint that was then possible, from that of the English merchant, for whom world trade was then opening up. In our view, this close connection of More with mercantile capital cannot be too strongly emphasised. To this we attribute the fact that More thought on modern lines, that his Socialism was of a modern kind.

We believe that we have disclosed the most essential roots of More's Socialism: his amiable character in harmony with primitive communism; the economic situation of England, which brought into sharp relief the disadvantageous consequences of capitalism for the working class; the fortunate union of classical philosophy with activity in practical affairs—all these circumstances combined must have induced in a mind so acute, so fearless, so truth-loving as More's an ideal which may be regarded as a foregleam of Modern Socialism.

2. *The Economic Criticism of " Utopia."*

More put forward his economic theories, but the time was not yet ripe for them.   But how keenly he observed the economic conditions of his time and how clearly he recognised the great principle, which forms one of the bases of modern Socialism, that man is a product of the material conditions in which he lives, and that a class of human beings can only be elevated through a corresponding change in the economic conditions, this he has proved in his *Utopia*, the critical parts of which even to-day possess more than an academic interest.

We cannot better indicate More's economic acumen, his boldness and likewise his amiability, than by letting him speak for himself.

We quote a passage from the first book of *Utopia* which contains a vivid description of the economic condition of England.   The passage forms an episode of the scene with Cardinal Morton from which we have already quoted some extracts throwing light upon More's ecclesiastical standpoint.

Raphael Hythloday is relating what happened to him when he visited Cardinal Morton in England.   " One day, when I was dining with him, there happened to be at table one of the English lawyers, who took occasion to run out in a high commendation of the severe execution of justice upon thieves, ' who,' as he said, ' were then hanged so fast that there were sometimes twenty on one gibbet !' and, upon that, he said, ' he could not wonder enough how it came to pass that, since so few escaped, there were yet so many thieves left, who were still robbing in all places.'

" Upon this, I (who took the boldness to speak freely before the Cardinal) said, ' There was no reason to wonder at the matter, since this way of punishing thieves was neither just in itself nor good for the public; for, as the severity was too great, so the remedy was not effectual; simple theft not being so great a crime that it ought to cost a man his life; no punishment, how severe soever, being able to restrain those from robbing who can find out no other way of livelihood. In this,' said I, 'not only you in England, but a great part of the world, imitate some ill masters, that are readier to chastise their scholars than to teach them. There are dreadful punishments enacted against thieves, but it were much better to make such good provisions by which each man might be put in a method how to live, and so be preserved from the fatal necessity of stealing and of dying for it.' 'There has been care enough taken for that,' said he; 'there are many handicrafts and there is husbandry, by which they may make a shift to live, unless they have a greater mind to follow ill courses.' 'That will not serve your turn,' said I, 'for many lose their limbs in civil or foreign wars, as lately in the Cornish rebellion, and some time ago in your Wars with France, who, being thus mutilated in the service of their king and country, can no more follow their old trades, and are too old to learn new ones; but since wars are only accidental things, and have intervals, let us consider those things that fall out every day. There is a great number of noblemen among you that are themselves as idle as drones, that subsist on other men's labour, on the labour of their tenants, whom, to raise their revenues, they pare to the quick. This, indeed, is the only instance of their frugality, for in all other things they are prodigal, even to the beggaring of themselves; but, besides this, they carry about with them a great number of idle fellows, who never learned any art by which they may gain their living; and these, as soon as either their lord dies, or they themselves fall sick, are turned out of doors; for your lords are readier to feed idle people than to take care of the sick; and often the heir is not able to keep together so great a family as his predecessor did.   Now, when the stomachs of those that are thus turned out of doors grow keen, they rob no less keenly; and what else can they do ? For when by wandering about, they have worn out both their health and their clothes, and are tattered, and look ghastly, men of quality will not entertain them, and poor men dare not do it, knowing that one who has been bred up in idleness and pleasure, and who was used to walk about with his sword and buckler, despising all the neighbour-hood with an insolent scorn as far below him, is not fit for the spade and mattock; nor will he serve a poor man for so small a hire and in so low a diet as he can afford to give him.'   To this he answered: 'This sort of men ought to be particularly cherished, for in them consists the force of the armies for which we have occasion, since their berth inspired them with a nobler sense of honour than is to be found among tradesmen and ploughmen.' 'You may as well say,' replied I, ' that you must cherish thieves on the account of wars, for you will never want the one as long as you have the other; and as robbers prove sometimes gallant soldiers, so soldiers often prove brave robbers, so near an alliance there is between these two sorts of life. But this bad custom, so common among you, of keeping many servants, is not peculiar to this nation. In France there is yet a more pestiferous sort of people, for the whole country is full of soldiers, still kept up in time of peace (if such a state of a nation can be called a peace); and these are kept in pay on the same account that you plead for those idle retainers about noblemen: this being a maxim of those pretended statesmen, that it is necessary for the public safety to have a good body of veteran soldiers ever in readiness. They think raw men are not to be depended on, and they sometimes seek

occasions for making war, that they may train up their
soldiers in the art of cutting throats, or, as Sallust observed,
" for keeping their hands in use, that they may not grow
dull by too long an intermission."   But France has learned
to its cost how dangerous it is to feed such beasts.   The
fate of the Romans, Carthaginians, and Syrians, and
many other nations and cities, which were both overturned
and quite ruined by those standing armies, should make
others wiser; and the folly of this maxim of the French
appears plainly even from this, that their trained soldiers
often find your raw men prove too hard for them, of which
I will not say much, lest you may think that I flatter
the English.   Every day's experience shows that the
mechanics in the towns or the clowns in the country are
not afraid of fighting with those idle gentlemen, if they
are not disabled by some misfortune in their body or
dispirited by extreme want; so that you need not fear
that those well-shaped and strong men (for it is only such
that noblemen love to keep about them till they spoil
them), who now grow feeble with ease and are softened
with their effeminate manner of life, would be less fit for
action if they were well bred and well employed.   And it
seems very unreasonable that, for the prospect of a war,
which you need never have but when you please, you
should maintain so many idle men, as will always disturb
you in time of peace, which is ever to be more considered
than war.   But I do not think that this necessity of
stealing arises only from hence; there is another cause of
it, more peculiar in England.'   'What is that ?' asked the
Cardinal.   'The increase of pasture,'said I, 'by which your
sheep which are naturally mild, and easily kept in order,
may be said to devour men and unpeople not only villages,
but towns; for wherever it is found that the sheep of any
soil yield a softer and richer wool than ordinary, there the
nobility and gentry, and even those holy men, the abbots,

not contented with the old rents which their farms yielded, not thinking it enough that they, living at their ease, do no good to the public, resolve to do it hurt instead of good. They stop the course of agriculture, destroying houses and towns, reserving only the churches, and enclose grounds that they may lodge their sheep in them. As if forests and parks had swallowed up too little of the land, those worthy countrymen turn the best inhabited places into solitudes; for when an insatiable wretch, who is a plague to his country, resolves to enclose many thousand acres of ground, the owners, as well as tenants, are turned out of their possessions by trick or by main force, or, being wearied out by ill usage, they are forced to sell them: by which means those miserable people, both men and women, married and unmarried, old and young, with their poor but numerous families (since country business requires many hands), are all forced to change their seats, not knowing whither to go; and they must sell, almost for nothing their household stuff, which could not bring them much money even though they might stay for a buyer. When that little money is at an end (for it will be soon spent), what is left for them to do but either to steal and so to be hanged (God knows how justly!) or to go about and beg, and if they do this they are put in prison as idle vagabonds, while they would willingly work but can find none that will hire them; for there is no more occasion for country labour, to which they have been bred, when there is no arable land left. One shepherd can look after a flock, which will stock an extent of ground that would require many hands if it were to be ploughed and reaped. This, likewise, in many places raises the price of corn. The price of wool is also so risen that the poor people, who were wont to make cloth, are no more able to buy it; and this, likewise, makes many of them idle; for since the increase of pasture God has punished the avarice of the owners by a rot among the sheep, which has destroyed vast numbers of them—to us it might have seemed more just had it fell on the owners themselves. But, suppose the sheep would increase ever so much, their price is not likely to fall, since, though they cannot be called a monopoly, because they are not engrossed by one person, yet they are in so few hands, that these are so rich that, as they are not pressed to sell them sooner than they have a mind to, so they never do it until they have raised the price as high as possible. And on the same account it is that the other kinds of cattle are so dear, because many villages being so pulled down, and all country labour being much neglected, there are none who make it their business to breed them. The rich do not breed cattle as they do sheep, but buy them lean and at low prices; and, after they have fattened them on their grounds, sell them again at high rates. And I do not think that all the inconveniences this will produce are yet observed; for, as they sell the cattle dear, so, if they are consumed faster than the breeding countries from which they are bought can afford them, then the stock must decrease, and this must needs end in great scarcity; and by these means, this your island, which seemed as to this particular the happiest in the world, will suffer much by the cursed avarice of a few persons; besides this, the rising of corn makes all people lessen their families as much as they can, and what do those who are dismissed by them do but either beg or rob? and to this last a man of a great mind is sooner drawn than by the former. Luxury likewise breaks in apace upon you to set forward your poverty and misery; there is an excessive vanity in apparel, and great cost in diet, and that not only in noblemen's families but even among tradesmen, among the farmers themselves, and among all ranks of persons. You have also many infamous houses, and besides those that are known the

12

taverns and ale-houses are no better; add to these dice, cards, tables, football, tennis, and quoits, in which money runs fast away; and those that are initiated in them must in conclusion betake themselves to robbing for a supply. Banish these plagues, and give orders that those who have dispeopled so much soil may either rebuild the villages they have pulled down or let out their grounds to such as will do it; restrain those engrossings of the rich, that are as bad almost as monopolies; leave fewer occasions to idleness; let agriculture be set up again, and the manufacture of the wool be regulated, that so there may be work found for those companies of idle people whom want forces to be thieves, or who now being idle vagabonds or useless servants will certainly grow thieves at last. If you do not find a remedy for these evils it is a vain thing to boast of your severity in punishing thieves, which though it may have the appearance of justice yet in itself is neither just or convenient; for if you suffer your people to be ill educated, and their manners to be corrupted from their infancy, and then punish them for those crimes to which their first education disposed them, what else is to be concluded from this but that you first make thieves and then punish them ?' ''

After More had put this severe criticism of the economic evils of his time into the mouth of his hero, Raphael Hythloday, he proceeds to discuss the best system of punishment.

In contrast to the cruel legislation of his time he proposed to punish theft, not by hanging or even imprisonment, but by compulsory labour.

A remarkable instance of clemency for the time.

This passage is followed by the political criticism which we have quoted in a previous chapter.

How are all those evils to be remedied ?

" Though to speak plainly my real sentiments, I must

freely own that as long as there is any property, and while
money is the standard of all other things, I cannot think
that a nation can be governed either justly or happily:
not justly, because the best things will fall to the worst
men; nor happily, because all things will be divided among
a few (and even these are not in all respects happy), the
rest being left to be absolutely miserable.   Therefore,
when I reflect on the wise and good constitution of the
Utopians, among whom all things are so well governed
and with so few laws, where virtue hath its due reward,
and yet there is such an equality that every man lives in
plenty, when I compare with them so many other nations
that are still making new laws, and yet can never bring
their constitution to a right regulation; where, notwithstanding every one has his property, yet all the laws that
they can invent have not the power either to obtain or
preserve it, or even to enable men certainly to distinguish
what is their own from what is another's, of which the
many lawsuits which every day break out, and are
eternally depending, give too plain a demonstration—
when, I say, I balance all these things in my thoughts,
I grow more favourable to Plato, and do not wonder
that he resolved not to make any laws for such as
would not submit to a community of all these things;
for so wise a man could not but foresee that the setting
all upon a level was the only way to make a nation
happy; which cannot be obtained so long as there is
property, for when every man draws to himself all that
he can compass, by one title or another, it must needs
follow that, how plentiful soever a nation may be, yet
a few dividing the wealth of it among themselves, the rest
must fall into indigence.   So that there will be two sorts
of people among them, who deserve that their fortunes
should be interchanged—the former useless, but wicked
and ravenous; and the latter who by their constant

industry serve the public more than themselves, sincere
and modest men—from whence I am persuaded that till
property is taken away, there can be no equitable or just
distribution of things, nor can the world be happily
governed; for as long as that is maintained the greatest
and the far best part of mankind will be still oppressed
with a load of cares and anxieties. I confess, without
taking it quite away, these pressures that lie on a great
part of mankind may be made lighter, but they can never
be quite removed; for if laws were made to determine at
how great an extent in soil, and at how much money, every
man must stop—to limit the prince, that he might not
grow too great; and to restrain the people, that they
might not become too insolent—and that none might
factiously aspire to public employments, which ought
neither be sold nor made burdensome by a great expense,
since otherwise those that serve in them would be tempted
to reimburse themselves by cheats and violence, and it
would become necessary to find out rich men for under-
going these employments, which ought rather to be
trusted to the wise. These laws, I say, might have such
an effect as good diet and care might have on a sick man
whose recovery is desperate; they might allay and mitigate
the disease, but it could never be quite healed, nor the
body politic be brought again to a good habit as long as
property remains; and it will fall out as in a complication
of diseases, that by applying a remedy to one sore you
will provoke another, and that which removes the one
ill symptom produces others, while the strengthening one
part of the body weakens the rest." "On the contrary,"
answered I, "it seems to me that men cannot live conveniently where all things are common. How can there
be any plenty where every man will excuse himself from
labour? for as the hope of gain doth not excite him so the
confidence that he has in other men's industry may make

him slothful. If people come to be pinched with want, and yet cannot dispose of anything as their own, what can follow upon this but perpetual sedition and bloodshed, especially when the reverence and authority due to magistrates falls to the ground ? for I cannot imagine how that can be kept up among those that are in all things equal to one another." "I do not wonder," said he, "that it appears so to you, since you have no notion, or at least no right one, of such a constitution; but if you had been in Utopia with me, and had seen their laws and rules, as I did, for the space of five years, in which I lived among them, and during which time I was so delighted with them that indeed I should never have left them if it had not been to make a discovery of that new world to the Europeans, you would then confess that you had never seen a people so well constituted as they."

This forms the connecting link with the description of More's ideal society.

3. *The Economic Tendencies of the Reformation in England.*

Before following our Communist into his Utopia, we must deal with a question which requires to be answered if our present enquiry is not to be incomplete: How is More's repugnance to every kind of exploitation to be reconciled with his defence of Catholicism, of exploitation by the monasteries and the Pope ?

The simple answer to this question is as follows: The exploitation of the people by Catholicism had become a slight thing in England at the time of More. The other side of Catholicism, the obstacle it presented to the impoverishment of the people, was much more emphasised. More could support Catholicism in his capacity as opponent of this impoverishment, quite apart from the political and Humanistic motives impelling him thereto which we have already discussed.

England had been one of the countries which was early exposed to papal exploitation in its severest form. But since the fourteenth century the dependence of England on the Papacy had been gradually disappearing, as we have shown in the fourth chapter of the second book, and consequently the exploitation of England by the Papal Stool had considerably diminished. The kings tolerated no more of it than they felt disposed. The popes could only extract money from England on condition of sharing the spoils with the kings. The " Holy Father " and the " Defender of the True Faith " haggled with each other like Polish Jews over their share in the proceeds of papal speculations in stupidity. In the case of the sale of indulgences, which was to give the impulse to the Reformation movement, the Pope offered Henry VIII. a quarter of the proceeds of the sale of indulgences in England, if Henry would give his permission for such sale, but Henry declared that he would be satisfied with nothing less than a third. Thus the indulgences became a new source of income for monarchs, a new tax, which the popes collected for them, taking on themselves, in return for a share, the full odium of the exploitation. As far as England was concerned the popes had become tax collectors for the king.

Not only the secular power, but also the clergy had become almost completely independent of the Papacy and refused to pay the ecclesiastical dues to Rome, when it did not suit either them or the monarchy. The same clergy who paid six-tenths to Henry VIII. refused in 1515 to grant even one-tenth to the Pope, who did not even prevail against them when he reduced his demand to one-half.

Consequently, so far as England was concerned, separation from the Papacy was in no way the sole means, as in Germany, of putting a stop to the exploitation of Rome. We must appraise More's attitude towards the German Reformation in the light of English conditions. More recognised at the outset that the Reformation could not remain an exclusively German affair, and Lutheranism soon penetrated to England. But what Lutheranism chiefly aimed at in England was not so much separation from the Papacy as the confiscation of the monasteries and pious endowments, which was demanded in numerous pamphlets. This in fact became, at a later date, the most powerful economic motive of Henry's ecclesiastical reformation. Henry was driven to this for political reasons: his defeat in the contest with Spain over the Pope, and for economic reasons: his growing need of money, which impelled him to lay hands on ecclesiastical property, when it had become impracticable and dangerous to increase taxation. He was encouraged to do so by his entourage: large landowners and land speculators, who were greedily looking forward to the time when ecclesiastical landed property should be given over to "free competition"—that is, the land robbers.

The Church owned a considerable area of land in England. A number of witnesses testify that the amount was one-third of the whole of the soil.

On this gigantic landed property the traditional mode of production lasted longer than on the other English estates. Feudalism was the economic foundation upon which the power and reputation of the monasteries was based. They clung to it as long as possible. They were, of course, obliged to make concessions to the uprising mode of production, but they did so reluctantly. In these compact corporations the traditions of feudalism retained greater vitality than among the newly created nobility who had succeeded the old nobles devoured by the Wars of the Roses. While the young noble plunged headlong into the stream of the capitalist development of his time and made greed for profit his chief passion, the monasteries continued to regard not only the extent of their land, but also the people settled thereon, as the basis of their power.

They frequently continued to cultivate a part of their land with numerous semi-feudal labourers, as they had done in the Middle Ages. They sought to attach their bondsmen by treating them well, and if they could no longer prevent their transformation into tenants, they strove to give them security by granting them unusually long leases. The monasteries therefore contributed but little to the impoverishment of the country people, and their estates were most thickly populated with peasants.

It may be imagined what the effect was to expose all these estates at one stroke to capitalist exploitation. Not only were the numerous inhabitants of the monasteries thrown into the ranks of the proletariat, but also the greater part of their tenants and settlers. The number of workless proletarians must have suddenly increased to an enormous degree.

The break-up of the monasteries also signified the collapse of the great medieval organisation for the relief of the poor; we have already discussed this rôle of the Church. In this respect England offered no special peculiarities. It is enough to say that the confiscation of the monasteries meant an increase in the number of the poor and at the same time the destruction of their last refuge.

More perceived that in Germany the first effect of the Reformation was that princes and nobles confiscated Church property; he noted that in England the Lutherans likewise clamoured most insistently for the confiscation of Church property; as an opponent of the impoverishment and exploitation of the country people he was obliged, in view of the peculiar economic situation of England, to declare against the Reformation.

And the demands of the Lutherans did not stop at the monasteries. They also demanded the confiscation of the property of the guilds. The greater part of the guild property that was invested in land, consisting mostly of endowments, served to maintain hospitals, schools, and almshouses for the support of impoverished guild members, for dowries, allowances for widows and orphans, and the like. It is easy to imagine what a powerful obstacle these endowments were to the impoverishment of handicraftsmen. In part they bore an ecclesiastical character, in accordance with the period in which they arose; they were bound up with provisions for the saying of masses, the maintenance of chapels, and the like. These provisions were seized hold of by the English Lutherans, in order to give a religious colouring to their greed for the guild property, and to demand its confiscation in order to suppress the " superstitious usages " which were connected with it.

Just as the champions of the confiscation of ecclesiastical and guild property based their demands not so much on economic as religious motives, so did their opponents adopt the same position. More, too, followed his antagonists into this sphere, and defended Church property and the pious endowments by a defence of masses (in his *Supplication of Souls*, 1529).

The contest over Church property was not decided until after its most energetic and capable champion had perished on the scaffold. A year after More's death the smaller monasteries were confiscated, in 1540 the large monasteries and abbeys. As, owing to Henry VIII.'s extravagance and the shameless deceptions of his creatures, these confiscations did not stop the leakage in the treasury and the most blatant debasements of the currency no longer availed, the bold step of destroying the guilds and confiscating their property was at length resorted to. A law with this object was passed in the last year of Henry's reign, but it was not enforced until the reign of his son Edward VI. Even then the powerful London guilds were not touched.

The English Reformation under Henry VIII. was a most audacious machination to intensify the exploitation of the people and enrich some of the most unprincipled creatures of the King. It had, therefore, no roots in the people, but rather aroused their increasing resentment. And when what More had foreseen and opposed actually came to pass, when the people felt the full force of the robbery that had been committed, the tendencies for which More had died gained the upper hand: under Edward VI., a formidable popular insurrection broke out against the Protestant Camarilla. It was, to be sure, defeated, but after Edward's death in 1553, the people set the Catholic Mary, Henry's daughter by his first wife, the Spanish Katherine, on the throne.

In opposing the Reformation, therefore, More did not act contrary to the interests of the exploited people. He owed his fate to the fact that he saw farther than the multitude, that he foresaw the consequences of the Reformation, of which the majority of the people did not become fully aware until a later date, and that he was obliged to pay with his life for his convictions at a time when they were not shared by a powerful section of the people.

Henry VIII.'s Reformation was not a protest against exploitation and responded to no popular need. Not until the reign of Bloody Mary did an economic antagonism develop between the English people and Catholicism, when the Reformation of Absolutism became invested with an economic interest for large classes of the people, and when that Protestantism was set in motion which brought so much popularity to Elizabeth in her efforts to enforce it.

The antagonism which won popular support for the Reformation in England was not between England and Rome, but between England and Spain. The exploitation of England by the Pope had, as we know, become insignificant even before Henry's Reformation. Consequently, the Pope was not hated so much in England as in Germany. But in the degree that England came to the front as a commercial State, in that degree did its interests become hostile to those of Spain, the great commercial power of the sixteenth century, which dominated the western seaboard of the Mediterranean and strove to be the mistress of the seas. Almost everywhere English commerce strove to develop, it found the road barred by Spain. It was strengthened in the constant struggle with the commerce of Spain, against which it conducted a guerilla war in the midst of peace; it was also strengthened by systematic piracy. From the coasts of the Iberian Peninsula to the North Sea English privateers were always loitering on the look-out for silver galleons from America or the rich merchant vessels carrying the treasures of the Indies from Lisbon to Antwerp, Portugal being a Spanish province from 1580 to 1640. Next to the slave trade, piracy was one of the foundations of England's commercial prosperity; both were officially encouraged. Elizabeth herself fitted out slave ships, vessels of the Navy engaged in piracy, and slave dealers and pirates, such as the famous world navigator, Francis Drake, were her favourites. Eventually Philip lost patience and equipped the great Armada to destroy piracy at its base, but it came to grief, as is well known, in the most disastrous fashion.

The outcome of the constant struggle for mastery of

the seas was boundless enmity and glowing hatred between the two nations.

In the sixteenth century the Spaniard was England's hereditary enemy, the prototype of everything horrible for a Briton. Now the Pope was a tool of Spain. To be Catholic was to be Spanish, was to serve the hereditary foe, was treason to the Motherland—that is, to her commercial interests.

Out of this antagonism grew the popular Protestantism of Elizabeth, and only thereby did the Reformation become a national fact, which under Henry VIII. had been, from the economic standpoint, a mere theft by an embarrassed prince and some equally embarrassed libertines and avaricious speculators.

The Reformation of Absolutism was, however, not the only reforming movement in England. Long before it a sect had formed which resisted exploitation not only by the Church, but also by the Church and the secular lords, which was therefore as hostile to the Royal Protestantism as to Catholicism. This sect struck firm roots among the poorer members of the community of whom More was the special champion, among the peasants and the small handicraftsmen and proletarians of the towns. Such were the Lollards, already mentioned, who adhered to the doctrines of Wiclif until they discovered in Calvinism a doctrine more congenial to them, whereupon they passed over to Puritanism. The Lollards had developed a kind of Socialism, but it was quite different from More's Socialism. The latter discloses itself as breathing, partly the fresh spirit of the feudal, primitive Catholicism, partly the joyous spirit of the aspiring bourgeoisie, serene and cultivated. The Socialism of the Lollards was the expression of a tortured, despairing class which had been crushed as much as possible. It was gloomy, ascetic, and barbaric.

If to this contrast we add More's repugnance to every

popular movement, it becomes plain that More could not be on friendly terms with the Lollards.

From his English standpoint he also condemned the German Anabaptists, who seemed to him half Lutherans and half Lollards.

His opinion of them was anything but favourable.

Thus he wrote to Johann Cochlaüs: "Germany daily produces more monsters than ever Africa did. What can be more monstrous than the Anabaptists? And yet, how has this plague spread within a few years!"

And in his *Confutation of Tyndall's Answer* (1532) he wrote: "And so ye may see that Tyndall affirmeth now not only those abominable heresies he taught before but all those also the Anabaptists have added unto them since. And so now be the true Church with him and agree with scripture and with the law of God, all those that say the baptising of children is void and that they say that there ought to be no rulers at all in Christendom neither spiritual nor temporal, and that no man should have anything proper of his own, but that all lands and all goods ought by God's law to be all men's in common, and that all women ought to be common to all men, as well the next of kin as the farthest stranger and every man husband to every woman and every woman wife unto every man and then finally that our blessed saviour Christ was but only man and not God at all."

The condemnation of communism as a "horrid heresy" by the communist More seems a strange inconsistence. Yet it is no chance personal phenomenon, but is bound up with the very essence of socialist beginnings. The antagonism between More and Münzer contains the seed of the great antagonism which runs through the entire history of Socialism, and which was only resolved by the Communist Manifesto, the antagonism between Utopianism and the Labour Movement.

The antagonism between More and Münzer, the theorist and the agitator, is essentially the same as that between Owenism and Chartism, between Fourierism and equalitarian communism in France.

However much More longed to see his ideal State realised he shuddered at every attempt to end exploitation from below. From his standpoint, therefore, communism would not develop in the class struggle by the logic of facts, it must be ready-made in the mind before one could think of inducing a powerful ruler to impose it on mankind from above.

That was an illusion. But to it More owed his supreme triumph, and we owe to it the first attempt to depict a mode of production which, while forming an alternative to the capitalist mode of production, at the same time retains the achievements which accompanied the triumph of capitalist civilisation over the preceding stage of development.

CHAPTER II

THE MODE OF PRODUCTION OF THE UTOPIANS

1. *Exposition.*

IN the second book of *Utopia* Raphael Hythloday describes the institutions and customs which obtain in the island of " Utopia " and which so delighted him. Let us first hear what he has to tell us regarding the mode of production, out of which arise the social, political, and religious institutions.

" There are fifty-four cities in the island of Utopia," relates Raphael, " all large and well built, the manners, customs, and laws of which are the same, and they are all contrived as near in the same manner as the ground on which they stand will allow. The nearest lie at least twenty-four miles' distance from one another, and the most remote are not so far distant but that a man can go on foot in one day from it to that which lies next it. . . . The jurisdiction of every city extends at least twenty miles, and where the towns lie wider, they have much more ground. No town desires to enlarge its bounds, for the people consider themselves rather as tenants than landlords.

" They have built, over all the country, farmhouses for husbandmen, which are well contrived, and furnished with all things necessary for country labour. Inhabitants are sent, by turns, from the cities to dwell in them; no country family has fewer than forty men and women in it, besides two bondmen.   There is a master and a mistress set over every family, and over thirty families there is a magistrate.

" Every year twenty of this family come back to the town after they have stayed two years in the country, and in their room there are other twenty sent from the town, that they may learn country work from those that have been already one year in the country, as they must teach those that come to them the next from the town.   By this means such as dwell in those country farms are never ignorant of agriculture, and so commit no errors which might otherwise be fatal and bring them under a scarcity of corn.   But though there is every year such a shifting of the husbandmen to prevent any man being forced against his will to follow that hard course of life too long, yet many among them take such pleasure in it that they desire leave to continue in it many years.

" These husbandmen till the ground, breed cattle, hew wood, and convey it to the towns either by land or water, as is most convenient.   They breed an infinite multitude of chickens in a very curious manner, etc.   And although they know exactly how much corn will serve every town and all that tract of country which belongs to it, yet they sow much more and breed more cattle than are necessary for their consumption, and they give the overplus of which they make no use to their neighbours.

" When they want anything in the country which it does not produce, they fetch that from the town, without carrying anything in exchange for it.   And the magistrates of the town take care to see it given them; for they meet generally in the town once a month, upon a festival day. When the time of harvest comes, the magistrates in the country send to those in the towns and let them know how many hands they will need for reaping the harvest; and the number they call for being sent to them, they commonly despatch it all in one day, when the weather is favourable."

So much for agriculture. Let us now turn to the town.

"The streets are very convenient for all carriage, and are well sheltered from the winds. Their buildings are good, and are so uniform that a whole side of a street looks like one house. The streets are twenty feet broad; there lie gardens behind all their houses. These are large, but enclosed with buildings, that on all hands face the streets, so that every house has both a door to the street and a back door to the garden. Their doors have all two leaves, which, as they are easily opened, so they shut of their own accord; and, there being no property among them, every man may freely enter into any house whatsoever. At every ten years' end they shift their houses by lots. They cultivate their gardens with great care, so that they have both vines, fruits, herbs, and flowers in them; and all is so well ordered and so finely kept that I never saw gardens anywhere that were both so fruitful and so beautiful as theirs. And this humour of ordering their gardens so well is not only kept up by the pleasure they find in it, but also by an emulation between the inhabitants of the several streets, who vie with each other. And there is, indeed, nothing belonging to the whole town that is both more useful and more pleasant.

"Agriculture is that which is so universally understood among them that no person, either man or woman, is ignorant of it; they are instructed in it from their childhood, partly by what they learn at school, and partly by practice, they being led out often into the fields about the town, where they not only see others at work but are likewise exercised in it themselves.

"Besides agriculture, which is so common to them all, every man has some peculiar trade to which he applies himself; such as the manufacture of wool or flax, masonry, smith's work, or carpenter's work; for there is no other sort of trade that is in great esteem among them.

"Throughout the island they wear the same sort of clothes, without any other distinction except what is necessary to distinguish the two sexes and the married and unmarried. The fashion never alters, and as it is neither disagreeable nor uneasy, so it is suited to the climate, and calculated both for their summers and winters. Every family makes their own clothes; but all among them, women as well as men, learn one or other of the trades formerly mentioned. Women, for the most part, deal in wool and flax, which suit best with their weakness, leaving the ruder trades to the men.

"The same trade generally passes down from father to son, inclinations often following descent: but if any man's genius lies another way he is, by adoption, translated into a family that deals in the trade to which he is inclined; and when that is to be done, care is taken, not only by his father, but by the magistrate, that he may be put to a discreet and good man: and if, after a person has learned one trade, he desires to acquire another, that is also allowed, and is managed in the same manner as the former. When he has learned both, he follows that which he likes best, unless the public has more occasion for the other.

"The chief, and almost the only, business of the Syphogrants is to take care that no man may live idle, but that every one may follow his trade diligently; yet they do not wear themselves out with perpetual toil from morning to night, as if they were beasts of burden, which as it is indeed a heavy slavery, so it is everywhere the common course of life amongst all mechanics except the Utopians; but they, dividing the day and night into twenty-four hours, appoint six of these for work, three of which are before dinner and three after; they then sup, and at eight o'clock, counting from noon, go to bed and sleep eight hours: the rest of their time, besides that taken up in work, eating, and sleeping, is left to every man's discretion.

"But the time appointed for labour is to be narrowly examined, otherwise you may imagine, that since there are only six hours appointed for work, they may fall under a scarcity of necessary provisions. But it is so far from being true, that this time is not sufficient for supplying them with plenty of all things, either necessary or convenient; that it is rather too much; and this you will easily apprehend, if you consider how great a part of all other nations is quite idle. First, women generally do little, who are the half of mankind; and if some few women are diligent, their husbands are idle: then consider the great company of idle priests, and of those that are called religious men; add to these all rich men, chiefly those that have estates in land, who are called noblemen and gentlemen, together with their families, made up of idle persons, that are kept more for show than use; add to these, all those strong and lusty beggars, that go about pretending some disease, in excuse for their begging; and upon the whole account you will find that the number of those by whose labours mankind is supplied, is much less than you perhaps imagined. Then consider how few of those that work are employed in labours that are of real service; for we who measure all things by money, give rise to many trades that are both vain and superfluous, and serve only to support riot and luxury. For if those who work were employed only in such things as the conveniences of life require, there would be such an abundance of them, that the prices of them would so sink, that tradesmen could not be maintained by their gains; if all those who labour about useless things, were set to more profitable employments, and if all they that languish out their lives in sloth and idleness, every one of whom consumes as much as any two of the men that are at work, were forced to labour, you may easily imagine that a small proportion of time would serve for doing all that is either necessary, profitable, or pleasant to mankind, especially while pleasure is kept within its due bounds. This appears very plainly in Utopia, for there, in a great city, and in all the territory that lies round it, you can scarce find five hundred, either men or women, by their age and strength, are capable of labour, that are not engaged in it; even the Syphogrants, though excused by the law, yet do not excuse themselves, but work, that by their examples they may excite the industry of the rest of the people. The like exemption is allowed to those, who being recommended to the people by the priests, are by the secret suffrages of the Syphogrants privileged from labour, that they may apply themselves wholly to study; and if any of these fall short of those hopes that they seemed at first to give, they are obliged to return to work. And sometimes a mechanic, that so employs his leisure hours as to make a considerable advancement in learning, is eased from being a tradesman, and ranked among their learned men. From these their officials are chosen.

" And thus from the great numbers among them that are neither suffered to be idle, nor to be employed in any fruitless labour, you may easily make the estimate how much may be done in those few hours in which they are obliged to labour. But besides all that has been already said, it is to be considered that the needful arts among them are managed with less labour than anywhere else. The building or the repairing of houses among us employ many hands, because often a thriftless heir suffers a house that his father built to fall into decay, so that his successor must, at a great cost, repair that which he might have kept up with a small charge: it frequently happens that the same house which one person built at a vast expense, is neglected by another, who thinks he has a more delicate sense of the beauties of architecture; and he suffering it to fall to ruin, builds another at no less charge. But among the Utopians, all things are so regulated that men very seldom build upon a new piece of ground; and are not only very quick in repairing their houses, but show their foresight in preventing their decay; so that their buildings are preserved very long, with but little labour; and thus the builders to whom that care belongs are often without employment, except the hewing of timber, and the squaring of stones, that the materials may be in readiness for raising a building very suddenly, when there is any occasion for it. As to their clothes, observe how little work is spent in them: while they are at labour, they are clothed with leather and skins, cast carelessly about them, which will last seven years; and when they appear in public they put on an upper garment, which hides the other; and these are all of one colour, and that is the natural colour of the wool. As they need less woollen cloth than is used anywhere else, so that which they make use of is much less costly. They use linen cloth more; but that is prepared with less labour, and they value cloth only by the whiteness of the linen, or the cleanness of the wool, without much regard to the fineness of the thread: while in other places, four or five upper garments of woollen cloth, of different colours, and as many vests of silk, will scarce serve one man; and while those that are nicer think ten too few, every man there is content with one, which very often serves him two years. Nor is there anything that can tempt a man to desire more; for if he had them, he would neither be the warmer, nor would he make one jot the better appearance of it. And thus, since they are all employed in some useful labour, and since they content themselves with fewer things, it falls out that there is a great abundance of all things among them: so that it frequently happens, that for want of other work, vast numbers are sent out to mend the highways. But when no public undertaking is to be performed, the hours of working are lessened. The magistrates never engage the people in unnecessary labour."

It is interesting to compare More's views with those of Marx regarding the curtailment of working hours in a communistic society. A similar train of thought will be found in both. In *Capital* we read: "Only by suppressing the capitalist form of production could the length of the working-day be reduced to the necessary labour-time. . . .

"The more the productiveness of labour increases, the more can the working-day be shortened; and the more the working-day is shortened, the more can the intensity of labour increase. From a social point of view, the productiveness increases in the same ratio as the economy of labour, which, in its turn, includes not only economy of the means of production, but also the avoidance of useless labour. The capitalist mode of production, while, on the one hand, enforcing economy in each individual business, on the other hand, begets, by its anarchical system of competition, the most outrageous squandering of labour-power and of the social means of production, not to mention the creation of a vast number of employments, at present indispensable, but in themselves superfluous.

"The intensity and productiveness of labour being given, the time which society is bound to devote to material production is shorter, and as a consequence, the time at its disposal for the free development, intellectual and social, of the individual is greater, in proportion as the work is more and more evenly divided among all the able-bodied members of society, and as a particular class is more and more deprived of the power to shift the natural burden of labour from its own shoulders to those of another layer of society. In this direction, the shortening of the working-day finds at last a limit in the generalisation of labour. In capitalist society spare time is acquired for one class by converting the whole life-time of the masses into labour-time " (*Capital*, vol. i., pp. 539-540).

So much for handicraft and agriculture in "Utopia." Both are occupations which possess a certain charm when not pursued to the point of weariness. The labour both of the handicraftsman and of the peasant is not monotonous, but full of variety. Each of them stands in a sort of personal relationship to the products of his labour, which are his pride and his joy. Of course, we are not thinking of the artisan and peasant in capitalist society, who are rather disguised proletarians, producers of surplus-value for the capitalists.

More was justified in assuming that agriculture and handicraft possess enough attraction in themselves to render any strict labour discipline unnecessary. But how does it fare with the unpleasant and repugnant kinds of labour ? To provide for their due performance, he invokes the aid of religion, which was still a powerful influence in his time.

" There are many among them (the Utopians) that upon a motive of religion neglect learning, and apply themselves to no sort of study; nor do they allow themselves any leisure time, but are perpetually employed, believing that by the good things that a man does he secures to himself that happiness that comes after death. Some of these visit the sick; others mend highways, cleanse ditches, repair bridges, or dig turf, gravel or stone. Others fell and cleave timber, and bring wood, corn, and other necessaries, on carts, into their towns; nor do these only serve the public, but they serve even private men, more than the slaves themselves do: for if there is anywhere a rough, hard, and sordid piece of work to be done, from which many are frightened by the labour and loathsomeness of it, they cheerfully, and of their own accord, take that to their share; and by that means, as they ease others very much, so they afflict themselves, and spend their whole life in hard labour: and yet they do not value themselves upon this, nor lessen other people's credit to raise their own; but by their stooping to such servile employments they are so far from being despised, that they are so much the more esteemed by the whole nation.

" Of these there are two sorts: some live unmarried and chaste, and abstain from eating any sort of flesh; and thus weaning themselves from all the pleasures of the present life, which they account hurtful, they pursue, even by the hardest and painfullest methods possible, that blessedness which they hope for hereafter; and the nearer they approach to it, they are the more cheerful and earnest in their endeavours after it.   Another sort of them is less willing to put themselves to much toil, and therefore prefer a married state to a single one; and as they do not deny themselves the pleasure of it, so they think the begetting of children is a debt which they owe to human nature, and to their country; nor do they avoid any pleasure that does not hinder labour; and therefore eat flesh so much the more willingly, as they find that by this means they are the more able to work: the Utopians look upon these as the wiser sect, but they esteem the other as the most holy."

These ideal, modest, enthusiastic labour monks, who stand in striking contrast to the lazy, dissolute and arrogant monks of More's time, do not, however, seem sufficient for the performance of unpleasant work, of which there were certain types which a pious man could not bring himself to do—for example, the slaughter of animals, work which inevitably brutalises those who perform it.   From such work More desired the Utopians to hold aloof.   But the work had to be done.   In this difficulty More was obliged to be false to himself, and to prescribe compulsory labour for one class of the inhabitants of Utopia.

" They do not make slaves of prisoners of war, except those that are taken in battle, nor of the sons of their slaves, nor of those of other nations: the slaves among them are only such as are condemned to that state of life for the commission of some crime, or, which is more common, such as their merchants find condemned to die in those parts to which they trade, whom they sometimes redeem at low rates, and in other places have them for nothing. They are kept at perpetual labour, and are always chained, but with this difference, that their own natives are treated much worse than the rest, and since they could not be restrained by the advantages of so excellent an education, are judged worthy of harder usage.

" Another sort of slaves are the poor of the neighbouring countries, who offer of their own accord to come and serve them: they treat these better, and use them in all other respects as well as their own countrymen, except their imposing more labour upon them, which is no hard task to those that have been accustomed to it; and if any of these have a mind to go back to their own country, which, indeed, falls out but seldom, as they do not force them to stay, so they do not send them away empty-handed."

But the position of the condemned criminal is not a hopeless one: " For the most part slavery is the punishment even of the greatest crimes, for as that is no less terrible to the criminals themselves than death, so they think the preserving them in a state of servitude is more for the interest of the commonwealth than killing them, since, as their labour is a greater benefit to the public than their death could be, so the sight of their misery is more lasting terror to other men than that which would be given by their death. If their slaves rebel, and will not bear their yoke and submit to the labour that is enjoined them, they are treated as wild beasts that cannot be kept in order, neither by a prison nor by their chains, and are at last put to death. But those who bear their punishment patiently, and are so much wrought on by that pressure that lies so hard on them, that it appears they are really more troubled for the crimes they have committed than for the miseries they suffer, are not out of hope, but that, at last, either the Prince will, by his prerogative, or the people, by their intercession, restore them again to their liberty, or, at least, very much mitigate their slavery."

The work of these bondsmen lies, among other things, in the slaughterhouse and the kitchen. From the slaughterhouses outside the town their beasts are brought into the towns, after they have been killed and prepared by the bondsmen; "for they suffer none of their citizens to kill their cattle, because they think that pity and good-nature, which are among the best of those affections that are born with us, are much impaired by the butchering of animals. . . . All the uneasy and sordid services about the dining-halls are performed by their slaves."

So much for work and the workers. We must now describe the economic relations of the whole community to the separate producing communities on the one hand, and to the outside world on the other.

" In their great council at Amaurot, to which there are three sent from every town once a year, they examine what towns abound in provisions and what are under any scarcity, that so the one may be furnished from the other; and this is done freely, without any sort of exchange; for, according to their plenty or scarcity, they supply or are supplied from one another, so that indeed the whole island is, as it were, one family. When they have thus taken care of their whole country, and laid up stores for two years (which they do to prevent the ill consequences of an unfavourable season), they order an exportation of the overplus, both of corn, honey, wool, flax, wood, wax, tallow, leather, and cattle, which they send out, commonly in great quantities, to other nations. They order a seventh part of all these goods to be freely given to the poor of the countries to which they send them, and sell the rest at moderate rates; and by this exchange they not only bring back those few things that they need at home (for, indeed, they scarce need anything but iron), but likewise a great deal of gold and silver; and by their driving this trade so long, it is not to be imagined how vast a treasure they have got among them." All neighbouring towns and States are indebted to them. The treasures are accumulated merely to permit the recruitment of mercenary troops and the bribing of a section of the enemy in the event of war.

They themselves have no money and thus require no gold, and to prevent any desire therefor arising, "they have fallen upon an expedient which, as it agrees with their other policy, so is it very different from ours, and will scarce gain belief among us who value gold so much, and lay it up so carefully. They eat and drink out of vessels of earth or glass, which make an agreeable appearance, though formed of brittle materials; while they make their chamber-pots and close-stools of gold and silver, and that not only in their public halls, but in their private houses. Of the same metals they likewise make chains and fetters for their slaves, to some of which, as a badge of infamy, they hang an earring of gold, and make others a chain or a coronet of the same metal."

Such is More's account of the economic relations of his ideal commonwealth.

2. *Criticism.*

Nobody with any knowledge of the subject would assert that More's aims are in complete agreement with the tendencies of modern scientific Socialism, which is based on two factors: the development of the proletariat as a class and the development of large-scale machine production, which enlists science in its service and to-day imposes a scheme of systematically organised social labour within each undertaking. Large-scale industry constitutes the technical foundation upon which, as modern Socialism holds, the proletariat will shape production in accordance with its interests, when it becomes a politically decisive factor.

The capitalist mode of production, however, developed its evils at an earlier time than it created the elements which are destined to remove them. The proletariat must become a permanent institution and an important section of the people before it is conscious of itself as a class and can reveal itself to the investigator as the power which will bear the burden of social reorganisation. On the other hand, under the system of commodity production, large-scale industry can only develop in the capitalistic form; it only became possible when large masses of capital had accumulated in a few hands, which were confronted with an army of propertyless, work-seeking proletarians.

Capital and proletariat, mass poverty and great wealth must exist for a long time before they develop the seeds of a new society. So long as such seeds are not disclosed, all attempts to remove the evils of the capitalist mode of production by the introduction of an alternative system are futile, and Socialism is doomed to remain of a Utopian character.

This was still the position at the beginning of the

nineteenth century. How much more unfavourable was it in More's time! At the beginning of the nineteenth century there was already a Labour Movement with definite aims; the only Labour Movement that More was acquainted with consisted of a few secret leagues and despairing revolts of artisan and peasant elements. At the beginning of the nineteenth century the transition from capitalist manufacture to large-scale industry could be clearly perceived. In More's time capitalism was just beginning to gain the upper hand over the industry and agriculture of England. Its domination had not lasted long enough to effect a technical revolution; the difference between capitalist and simple commodity production was of degree rather than of kind. The worker who wove wool for the merchant did so in the same way as the members of the Weavers' Guild. The difference consisted merely in the fact that the merchant employed more workers than the master weaver, and that the master weaver's journeymen had every prospect of becoming masters themselves, while the wage worker of the capitalist merchant had no chance of ever becoming a capitalist. The distinction between the capitalist and the guild mode of production was then only of a social, not of a technical character: handicraft was the basis of one as of the other.

Agriculture was in a like case. The undertakings of capitalist farmers were at first distinguished from those of feudal settlers by their magnitude. There was little to be seen of improvements in methods of cultivation or the use of perfected tools. Men were made superfluous, not by an increase in the productivity of agricultural labour, but by the transition to a ruder form of agricultural production, from cornfields to pasturage.

However obvious, therefore, certain of the evils of capitalism were in More's time, the technical foundations upon which it was based, and upon which More was obliged to build up his anti-capitalist commonwealth, were still handicraft and peasant agriculture.

It is clear that More could not avoid deviating in many points from modern Socialism. Reactionary as he seems to us in many respects, if one is so foolish as to measure him by the standards of the twentieth and not by the sixteenth century—being, in consequence of the backwardness of the proletariat, an opponent of every popular movement and a champion of constitutional monarchy—More's Socialism often appears retrogressive in an economic respect. The surprising thing is, however, that in spite of the unfavourable conditions, More's Socialism does exhibit so many of the most essential features of modern Socialism that he may rightly be counted among modern Socialists.

The unmodern aspects of More's Communism are the necessary consequences of the mode of production he was obliged to take as his starting-point. The chief of these reactionary features is the attachment of every man to a specific handicraft.

The most important work in modern large-scale industry is assigned to science, which methodically investigates the mechanical and chemical forces employed in production, and also investigates the mechanical and chemical properties of the various materials whose transformation is the object of production, and finally directs the application of the technical principles it has investigated. Only a few easily learned movements in connection with supervising the machinery or the chemical processes are left to the hand worker.

This vacuity and simplicity of manual labour is to-day one of the most important causes of its degrading tendency. It no longer employs or attracts the mind, and is repellent and blunting in its effect. It permits skilled labour to be replaced by unskilled, and strong workers by weak workers.

It also frees the capitalists to an increasing extent from the necessity of keeping a staff of skilled workers. And simultaneously the conditions of production are constantly being transformed by the application of science to production, for science does not rest, nor does the pressure of competition to effect new improvements. The machine of yesterday is obsolete to-day, and out of the running to-morrow.

When the proletariat directs production, it will transform these causes of the degradation of the working class into so many instruments for its elevation. The simplification of machine movements renders it possible for the worker to change his work from time to time, bringing into play a number of muscles and nerves whose harmonious activity will impart vitality just as unproductive gymnastics do to-day. Successively engaged in the most diverse occupations, he will then become conscious of his latent capabilities, and from a machine will become a free man. And the simultaneous preoccupation with the sciences, which will come with a shorter working day, will restore intellectual meaning to his work, by disclosing its connection with the totality of technical and economic processes and their roots.

Instead of changes of work, which is only possible with large-scale production, and will also be necessary if the working class is not to degenerate, More prescribes the attachment of every worker to a specific handicraft. In handicraft the handling of the tool and the knowledge of its effect upon the raw material is not the result of methodical and scientific investigation, but is the accumulation of personal, often haphazard, experiences. This is also the case with manufacture, where, however, each division of production is split up into various detail processes, to each of which a worker is permanently assigned, and to learn which does not, of course, require as much time as is necessary to learn all the movements and methods of a specific process of production. While it is necessary in manufacture to keep a worker for a long time at his detail process, in order to acquire the needful skill to make his labour as productive as possible, in handicraft it is a technical necessity to put a worker to a certain trade in youth, so that from constant intercourse with a skilled master, he may become acquainted with all the traditions of the trade. This apprenticeship did not appear an evil, as handicraft still possessed a certain charm.

But how shall we deal with the work of day labourers, who were already very numerous in More's time, with the dirty work—slaughtering, sanitary services, etc.? These unpleasant labours, a favourite objection of the Philistine to Socialism, have been a thorn in the flesh for all Utopists. Fourier tried to solve the problem by introducing psychological motives, often very ingeniously contrived, into work. More attempted to achieve something similar, as we have seen, by the lever of religion, which was so strong in his time. But as he did not consider this sufficient, he was obliged to have recourse to the compulsory labour of slaves, and to introduce into his commonwealth a class without property and rights working for others. He resorts to all kinds of devices to soften this institution by pointing to persons in that class who might otherwise have been overtaken by a worse fate. To remove the degraded class entirely was impossible for him, given the technical foundation of his speculations. Only modern large-scale industry provides the full opportunity for adjusting the various kinds of work, and so simplifying the residue of unpleasant work as to permit of its alternate performance by all capable of labour, thus abolishing any special compulsion upon an unfortunate class of workers. The distinction between pleasant and unpleasant work has largely disappeared, inasmuch as work which was formerly pleasant has been divested of every attraction. But modern technology has also succeeded in lightening or abolishing many unpleasant tasks. On the whole, however, technology has not hitherto accomplished very much in this direction. To make work more pleasant is not the task which capitalism assigns to it. Capitalism desires a saving of labour-power, even though the unpleasantness of work be increased. Only when the working class exercises a decisive influence upon the mode of production, will science be utilised to throw its whole weight into solving the problem of abolishing unpleasant labours. And there is no problem of this kind which modern technology could not solve as soon as it seriously applied itself thereto. Moreover, a great part of the unpleasant work of to-day will be abolished by the transfer of industry to the countryside, of which we shall have to speak.

A third feature which contradicts modern Socialism may be referred to in this connection: the frugality of the Utopians.

More's intention is—and this is quite a modern feature—to free the citizens of his commonwealth as much as possible from physical labour, in order to procure them leisure for intellectual and social activity. His chief means to this end are the organisation of labour, to avoid all the useless work which the existing anarchy introduces into the economic life, and which was comparatively slight in More's time, and finally the restriction of wants.

The first two points More has in common with modern Socialism, but not the last. To speak to-day of the necessity of restricting wants, in order to shorten working hours, would imply a strange misconception of the conditions of our age of over-production, where one technical improvement follows another, where the mode of production has reached such a level of productivity that it threatens to burst the framework of capitalism, in order to develop without hindrance.

It was different in More's time. The productivity of handicraft developed very slowly, and sometimes completely ossified. And so it was with peasant agriculture. No considerable increase of production in relation to the number of workers could be expected from a communism established on this foundation. Consequently, wants had to be limited if it was desired to reduce hours of labour.

The effect of capitalism, as More saw it, was not over-production, but scarcity. Pasturage was extended at the expense of agriculture, resulting in a rise in the prices of food, which was partly caused by the flow of silver and gold from America to Europe. What, however, was of greater weight with More in making his Utopians of frugal manners was the senseless luxury of his age. A luxury in clothing as in the furnishing of houses, an excessive pomp, developed, which served not for the satisfaction of an artistic need, but the display of wealth. It is easy to understand why More combated this with great vigour, and why he went to the opposite extreme in clothing his Utopians with skins and uniform woollen garments.

Do not, however, believe that More preached a monkish asceticism. On the contrary, we shall see him revealed as a true Epicurean in respect of harmless enjoyments which did not impose superfluous work upon the community.

Here, as elsewhere, his unmodern ideas appear as limitations imposed upon him by the backwardness of his age, without influencing him to the extent of obscuring the essentially modern character of his ideals.

This becomes obvious when we consider what features More's Socialism has in common with present-day Socialism, in contrast both to primitive communism, with whose vestiges More became acquainted, and to Plato's communism, with which, as we know, he was familiar.

We have already noted how world commerce broke down the exclusiveness and restrictions of the primitive community, beyond which even Plato did not advance, as he put the nation as an economic unity in place of the village community.

But world trade also broke down the caste system of the primitive communities.

Like the medieval towns, the Platonic Republic was divided into rigidly defined castes, and Plato's communism was a privilege of the supreme caste.

On the other hand, the vital principle of capitalism is free competition: equality of competitive conditions for everybody, and therefore abolition of caste distinctions. If capitalism united the small communities into a nation, it also tended to absorb all castes into one nation.

This tendency of capitalism also coincides with More's communism. It is national in contrast to the local and caste communism of the past, with which More was acquainted by experience and study. In this, he was more modern than present-day Anarchism, which aims at splitting up the nation into independent groups and communes.

We have seen that the Senate of the Utopians consists of delegates from the various communities; it is this representative body of the nation which organises production, estimates the needs which it is to supply, and divides the labour produce according to the results of these statistics. The local communities are not commodity producers, exchanging their products for those of other communities. Each one produces for the whole nation. The nation, and not the local community, is also the owner of the means of production; above all, of the land.

And not the local community, but the Commonwealth as a whole sells to foreign countries the superfluity of products and receives the proceeds of such sale. Gold and silver constitute the war chest of the nation.

The equality of all members of the community, however, which under capitalism only implies an equality of competitive conditions, becomes, under More's communism, an equal obligation of all to labour. This great principle connects it most closely with modern Socialism, and distinguishes it most sharply from Plato's communism, which is a communism of non-workers, of exploiters. The privileged class of the Platonic Republic, the "guardians," who alone practise communism, regarded work as something degrading; they lived on the tribute from the working citizens.

There is only one unimportant exception from the equal obligation to labour in *Utopia*: among the able-bodied a few scholars are exempted. This exception was necessary under the system of handicraft, where manual work was too onerous to leave time for mental activity.

The existence of compulsory labour, of course, contravenes the equality of the Utopians. We have seen what the explanation of this contradiction is. Moreover, More himself, in making this concession to the backwardness of the contemporary mode of production, preserved the modern character as much as possible, inasmuch as he made the bondsmen, not a hereditary caste, but a class. The bondsmen are either foreign wage workers, who may change their position if they desire, or declassed persons condemned to forced labour, owing to their misconduct, with the chance of retrieving their characters.

Specially noteworthy and completely in line with present-day Socialism is the equal obligation to work imposed on man and woman, the assigning to woman an industrial vocation.   Women as well as men must learn a handicraft.   We shall revert to the subject of woman's work in the next chapter.

An important and characteristic feature of the mode of production of the Utopians has yet to be mentioned: the removal of the antagonism between town and country.

This problem is a wholly modern one, due to the concentration of industry in the towns.   In More's time the solution of the problem was not so pressing as it is to-day.   Yet the antagonism between town and country had already developed pretty considerably in many countries.   This may be inferred from the rise of pastoral poetry (first in Italy in the fifteenth century) which expressed the longing of the townsman for the country.

More had a particularly good opportunity to observe the tendency of the modern mode of production to increase the size of the great towns, for London was one of the most rapidly growing towns of that time.

More himself left London as often as he could to stay in the village of Chelsea.

The conditions of London and More's own inclinations combined to convince him of the necessity for abolishing the antagonism between town and country.

This can only be done by transferring industry to the countryside, by combining industrial with agricultural labour.   If, however, this adjustment is not to lead to general rustication, the technical means must exist to remove that isolation which is necessarily bound up with small peasant farming, means for the communication of ideas by other methods than personal intercourse— newspapers, post, telegraph, telephone, must be highly developed, as well as means for the transport of products, machines, raw materials, and persons: railways, steamers, motor traffic.   Finally, every agricultural undertaking must be so extensive as to permit of the concentration of a larger number of workers in one spot.

All these preliminary conditions were entirely absent in More's time. His aim, however, was a higher level of mental culture, not the rustication of the whole people. This combination of agricultural with industrial labour was, therefore, impossible for him, and he was obliged to content himself with prescribing a certain period of agricultural labour for every citizen, making children familiar with it from an early age, and setting a limit to the size of the towns. We shall learn that no town might number more or less than 6,000 families, comprising ten to sixteen adults. These devices do not, of course, harmonise with modern Socialism, but they were a necessity imposed upon More by the small-scale production of his time.

We observe again that More's aims are modern, but their realisation was prevented by the backwardness of the mode of production of his time. This was sufficiently developed to enable an observer like More, methodically trained and specially cognisant of the economic conditions, and under the particularly favourable circumstances which England then offered, to perceive its tendencies, but not far enough developed to disclose the means of overcoming these tendencies.

Thus More's communism is modern in most of its tendencies, and unmodern in most of its expedients.

CHAPTER III

THE FAMILIES OF THE UTOPIANS

1. *Description.*

THE mode of production determines the type of the household, and the latter determines the forms of the family and of marriage, as well as the position of woman. Let us see how More would organise these relationships in his ideal commonwealth. In this connection his attitude towards the population question may be dealt with.

"As their cities are composed of families, so their families are made up of those that are nearly related to one another. Their women, when they grow up, are married out, but all the males, both children and grandchildren, live still in the same house, in great obedience to their common parent, unless age has weakened his understanding, and in that case he that is next to him in age comes in his room; but lest any city should become either too great, or by any accident be dispeopled, provision is made that none of their cities may contain above six thousand families, besides those of the country around it. No family may have less than ten and more than sixteen persons in it, but there can be no determined number for the children under age; this rule is easily observed by removing some of the children of a more fruitful couple to any other family that does not abound so much in them. By the same rule they supply cities that do not increase so

215

fast from others that breed faster; and if there is any increase over the whole island, then they draw out a number of their citizens out of the several towns and send them over to the neighbouring continent, where, if they find that the inhabitants have more soil than they can well cultivate, they fix a colony, taking the inhabitants into their society if they are willing to live with them; and where they do that of their own accord, they quickly enter into their method of life and conform to their rules, and this proves a happiness to both nations; for, according to their constitution, such care is taken of the soil that it becomes fruitful enough for both, though it might be otherwise too narrow and barren for any one of them.   But if the natives refuse to conform themselves to their laws they drive them out of those bounds which they mark out for themselves, and use force if they resist, for they account it a very just cause of war for a nation to hinder others from possessing a part of that soil of which they make no use, but which is suffered to lie idle and uncultivated, since every man has, by the law of nature, a right to such a waste portion of the earth as is necessary for his subsistence.   If an accident has so lessened the number of the inhabitants of any of their towns that it cannot be made up from the other towns of the island without diminishing them too much (which is said to have fallen out but twice since they were first a people, when great numbers were carried off by the plague), the loss is then supplied by recalling as many as are wanted from their colonies, for they will abandon these rather than suffer the towns in the island to sink too low.

" But to return to their manner of living in society: the oldest man of every family, as has been already said, is its governor; wives serve their husbands, and children their parents, and always the younger serves the elder.

Every city is divided into four equal parts, and in the middle of each there is a market-place. What is brought thither, and manufactured by the several families, is carried from thence to houses appointed for that purpose, in which all things of a sort are laid by themselves; and thither every father goes, and takes whatsoever he or his family stand in need of, without either paying for it or leaving anything in exchange. There is no reason for giving a denial to any person, since there is such plenty of everything among them; and there is no danger of a man's asking for more than he needs; they have no inducements to do this, since they are sure they shall always be supplied: it is the fear of want that makes any of the whole race of animals either greedy or ravenous; but, besides fear, there is in man a pride that makes him fancy it a particular glory to excel others in pomp and excess; but by the laws of the Utopians, there is no room for this.''

Near these markets were the provision markets, where cattle was brought already slaughtered and purified, as we have seen. The slaughtering was done outside the town by a brook, to spare the town the infection of ill-smells.

''In every street there are great halls, that lie at an equal distance from each other, distinguished by particular names. The Syphogrants dwell in those that are set over thirty families, fifteen lying on one side of it, and as many on the other. In these halls they all meet and have their repasts; the stewards of every one of them come to the market-place at an appointed hour, and according to the number of those that belong to the hall they carry home provisions. But they take more care of their sick than of any others; who are lodged in hospitals situated without every town, and so conveniently appointed that every sick person prefers treatment in the hospital to remaining at home.

"At the hours of dinner and supper the whole Sypho-granty being called together by sound of trumpet, they meet and eat together, except only such as are in the hospitals or lie sick at home. Yet, after the halls are served, no man is hindered to carry provisions home from the market-place, for they know that none does that but for some good reason; for though any that will may eat at home, yet none does it willingly, since it is both ridiculous and foolish for any to give themselves the trouble to make ready an ill dinner at home when there is a much more plentiful one made ready for him so near hand. All the uneasy and sordid services about these halls are performed by their slaves; but the dressing and cooking their meat, and the ordering of their tables, belong only to the women, all those of every family taking it by turns. They sit at three or more tables, according to their number; the men sit towards the wall, and the women sit on the other side, that if any of them should be taken suddenly ill, which is no uncommon case amongst women with child, she may, without disturbing the rest, rise and go to the nurses' room (who are there with the sucking children), where there is always clean water at hand and cradles, in which they may lay the young children if there is occasion for it, and a fire, that they may shift and dress them before it. Every child is nursed by its own mother if death or sickness does not intervene; and in that case the Syphogrants' wives find out a nurse quickly, which is no hard matter, for any one that can do it offers herself cheerfully; for as they are much inclined to that piece of mercy, so the child whom they nurse considers the nurse as its mother. All the children under five years old sit among the nurses; the rest of the younger sort of both sexes, till they are fit for marriage, either serve those that sit at table, or, if they are not strong enough for that, stand by them in great silence and eat what is given them; nor have they any other formality of dining.''

This is followed by a detailed account of the common meal times, which we must omit, as it contains nothing essential and important and would take us too far out of our way. The description concludes in the following manner:

"They despatch their dinners quickly, but sit long at supper, because they go to work after the one, and are to sleep after the other, during which they think the stomach carries on the concoction more vigorously. They never sup without music, and there is always fruit served up after meat; while they are at table some burn perfumes and sprinkle about fragrant ointments and sweet waters—in short, they want nothing that may cheer up their spirits; they give themselves a large allowance that way, and indulge themselves in all such pleasures as are attended with no inconvenience. Thus do those that are in the towns live together; but in the country, where they live at a great distance, every one eats at home, and no family wants any necessary sort of provision, for it is from them that provisions are sent unto those that live in the towns.''

So much for the household of the Utopians. Their marriage customs are described in the chapter on slavery: "Their women are not married before eighteen nor their men before two-and-twenty, and if any of them run into forbidden embraces before marriage they are severely punished, and the privilege of marriage is denied them unless they can obtain a special warrant from the Prince. Such disorders cast a great reproach upon the master and mistress of the family in which they happen, for it is supposed that they have failed in their duty. The reason of punishing this so severely is, because they think that if they were not strictly restrained from all vagrant appetites, very few would engage in a state in which they venture the quiet of their whole lives, by being confined to one person, and are obliged to endure all the inconveniences with which it is accompanied. In choosing their wives they use a method that would appear to us very absurd and ridiculous, but it is constantly observed among them, and is accounted perfectly consistent with wisdom. Before marriage some grave matron presents the bride, naked, whether she is a virgin or a widow, to the bridegroom, and after that some grave man presents the bridegroom, naked, to the bride. We, indeed, both laughed at this, and condemned it as very indecent. But they, on the other hand, wondered at the folly of the men of all other nations, who, if they are but to buy a horse of a small value, are so cautious that they will see every part of him, and take off both his saddle and all his other tackle, that there may be no secret ulcer hid under any of them, and that yet in the choice of a wife, on which depends the happiness or unhappiness of the rest of his life, a man should venture upon trust, and only see about a hand's-breadth of the face, all the rest of the body being covered, under which may lie hid what may be contagious as well as loathsome. All men are not so wise as to choose a woman only for her good qualities, and even wise men consider the body as that which adds not a little to the mind, and it is certain there may be some such deformity covered with clothes as may totally alienate a man from his wife, when it is too late to part with her; if such a thing is discovered after marriage a man has no remedy but patience; they, therefore, think it is reasonable that there should be good provision made against such mischievous frauds.

" There was so much the more reason for them to make a regulation in this matter, because they are the only people of those parts that neither allow of polygamy nor of divorces, except in the case of adultery or insufferable perverseness, for in these cases the Senate dissolves the marriage and grants the injured person leave to marry again; but the guilty are made infamous and are never allowed the privilege of a second marriage. None are suffered to put away their wives against their wills, from any great calamity that may have fallen on their persons, for they look on it as the height of cruelty and treachery to abandon either of the married persons when they need most the tender care of their consort, and that chiefly in the case of old age, which, as it carries many diseases along with it, so it is a disease of itself. But it frequently falls out that when a married couple do not well agree, they, by mutual consent, separate, and find out other persons with whom they hope they may live more happily; yet this is not done without obtaining leave of the Senate, which never admits of a divorce but upon a strict enquiry made, both by the senators and their wives, into the grounds upon which it is desired, and even when they are satisfied concerning the reasons of it they go on but slowly, for they imagine that too great easiness in granting leave for new marriages would very much shake the kindness of married people. They punish severely those that defile the marriage bed; if both parties are married they are divorced, and the injured persons may marry one another, or whom they please, but the adulterer and the adulteress are condemned to slavery, yet if either of the injured persons cannot shake off the love of the married person they may live with them still in that state, but they must follow them to that labour to which the slaves are condemned, and sometimes the repentance of the condemned, together with the unshaken kindness of the innocent and injured person, has prevailed so far with the Prince that he has taken off the sentence; but those that relapse after they are once pardoned are punished with death.''

To this account a few sentences may be added which throw light on the position of women in Utopia. "Husbands have power to correct their wives and parents to chastise their children, unless the fault is so great that a public punishment is thought necessary for striking terror into others."

"But as they force no man to go into any foreign war against his will, so they do not hinder those women who are willing to go along with their husbands; on the contrary, they encourage and praise them, and they stand often next their husbands in the front of the army. They also place together those who are related, parents, and children, kindred, and those that are mutually allied, near one another; that those whom nature has inspired with the greatest zeal for assisting one another may be the nearest and readiest to do it; and it is a matter of great reproach if husband or wife survive one another, or if a child survives his parent."

"The wives of their priests are the most extraordinary women of the whole country; sometimes the women themselves are made priests, though that falls out but seldom, nor are any but ancient widows chosen into that order."

These quotations suffice to describe the marriage and family customs of the Utopians.

2. *Criticism.*

We have already shown in what amiable detail the common meals of the Utopians are described. This is not chance, nor More's personal predilection, but is part of the essence of his Communism. Large-scale industry, which is the starting-point of modern Socialism, is a system of social labour; a large-scale undertaking requires the systematic co-operation of hundreds, even thousands, of men, women, and children. What modern Socialism aims at is the extension of this social character of work within the individual undertaking to the whole field of production, and the adaptation of the mode of appropria‧tion to the mode of production. The partially social character of work as it exists to-day is the starting-point of the communistic character of the commonwealth which modern Socialism labours to achieve.

Handicraft and peasant agriculture, which formed More's starting-point, on the contrary, imply the isolation of numerous small concerns. Consequently, More was obliged to lay all the greater stress upon the social character of meals and pleasures. Sociality in this sphere is a point of secondary importance for modern Socialism, but a vital condition for More's Socialism. In this respect, More has closer affinity with the so-called socialistic phenomena of Antiquity, above all, with Platonic Communism, than with present-day Socialism.

The common meals, however, were important for More not only as a means of cementing social cohesion, but as a partial means of emancipating woman from household labours.

This brings us to an aspect of the question which generally furnished a good test for the character of a socialistic system.

The starting-point of modern proletarian Socialism is large-scale industry, a mode of production which trans-forms the various branches of work of the individual household into public services.

Women's work in the home becomes not only increas-ingly superfluous, but also an increasingly intolerable burden, both for the wife and the husband.

Simultaneously, large-scale industry increases the opportunities and the advantages of employing women in industry. Women are thus drawn away from the narrowness and isolation of their households into a wider life.

The emancipation of women from the household involves their political emancipation. An equal footing for the sexes in public life is advocated by every modern proletarian socialist, as it was by the great Utopians.

In this respect More anticipated a principle of modern Socialism before the material conditions existed upon which this principle could be based.

By his ordinance of common meals More only partially achieved the emancipation of women from the separate household, as he had perforce to leave one of its strongest supports standing: the peasant and handicraft mode of production, which determined that a separate household should correspond to every separate unit of production, as was typically developed in the Roman family. The Roman word *familia* signifies, in fact, not the whole of the blood relatives, but the whole of those allied in a specific unit of production.

It was natural that the wife and children of a peasant should work with him in tilling the land, tending the cattle, etc., and, of course, his grandchildren when the size of the concern required it. But the slaves who, in addition to these relatives, were employed in the undertaking, likewise belonged to the Roman family. Children who left the concern, such as daughters to be married, ceased to belong to the family. The head of the family was the director of the undertaking, and as such the members of the family owed him unquestioning obedience. The children of the Roman family occupied the same position towards him as the slaves, and it is characteristic that the son could only become free from the supremacy of the father by being sold by him, at least in appearance, as a slave.

The patriarchal peasant family and household of the

Middle Ages was organised in a similar manner, although its divisions were not so rigid. All those who took part in the direction of a separate peasant undertaking formed an economic unit.

Even with medieval handicraft every undertaking formed a household, a family in itself, excluding the children of the master engaged in other undertakings, but including the apprentices and journeymen, whether or not they were related to the master. Many trade secrets were family secrets, handed down from father to son. Sometimes the business was exclusively confined to the family (in the sense of blood-relationship). In the case of the medieval handicraftsman, as in that of the peasant, the business and the household were closely bound up with each other.

On the other hand, a typical capitalist business is quite separate from the household of its owner and manager. This allows the wage workers to set up a home of their own, which the guild journeymen could not do, but it also permits the workers to starve while the master lives in luxury, whereas under guild handicraft both feasted at the same table. As capitalism reacted upon handicraft, the unity of business and household was gradually broken down. With the peasant, however, it has generally lasted until to-day.

In More's time the household both in agriculture and industry was still firmly attached to the business.

Although More loosened this attachment by his common meals, so far as the town workers were concerned, he could not entirely sever it. Consequently, we find the patriarchal family in his pages in almost classical form. The families of the Utopians are productive associations, like the handicraft families of the Middle Ages, connected for the most part by ties of blood. The size of these families is determined by technical considerations. The

15

peasant families are larger than the handicraft families; the former number at least forty, the latter only ten to sixteen adults. Redundant members of one family fill the gap in another family.

When More grafted the patriarchal family on to his Utopian commonwealth, he could not escape its consequences, although he tried to neutralise them as much as possible, so far as they were unfavourable to women.

He not only left intact a certain degree of subordination of the wife to the husband, but also preserved the forms of sexual relationships peculiar to the patriarchal family—the requirement of pre-nuptial maiden chastity, and strict prohibition of adultery. These prescriptions were so deeply rooted that they have undergone little change in the last four centuries, and it was difficult for More to escape their influence. The most he could do was to soften the harshness of marriage relationships. But in some respects he has even accentuated this strictness, by extending the limitations imposed on women to men, instead of giving women the freedom of men. Thus he requires both sexes to observe pre-nuptial chastity, and forbids either to commit adultery. In respect of divorce, he introduces some trifling relaxations. Yet he requires that marriage should rest on mutual inclination, a necessary provision if the wife is not to be the slave of the husband, and if the latter is to be forbidden extra-marital intercourse. To obviate subsequent repentance and desire for divorce, he adopts the expedient of introducing bride and bridegroom to each other in a nude state.

Such hair-splitting is the necessary result of the attempt to explore the possibilities of realising an idea, while the actual conditions were only developed far enough to give an impulse to this idea, without providing the conditions necessary for its realisation.

In his analysis of the family and marriage More's genius

encountered more difficulties from the actual conditions which surrounded him than in his analysis of the mode of production. Consequently, we find in the former to a greater extent than in the latter principles peculiar to modern Socialism mixed up with those that belong to a past mode of production, and a past form of the family. The principle of common meals, the participation of women in public life, in war and in the priesthood, as well as in the choice of officials, are modern principles, while the maintenance of the subordination of woman and of the patriarchal separate household conflict with the tendencies of modern Socialism, and even with the tendencies of More's own Socialism.

He has little in common with Plato in the sphere we are discussing. It is difficult to decide whether More was ever enthusiastic for the community of women. Erasmus, who tells us this, understood More's Socialism too little to rank as a trustworthy source of information on this question. We know that in *Utopia* More advocated strict monogamy and the free choice of partners, and was thus in direct conflict with Plato, who advocates the community of women and sexual selection from above, both of which institutions run counter to modern feeling.

If More is farther from Plato than from us in this respect, both are much alike, and deviate from modern Socialism, in their attitude towards the population question. They both consider it necessary for the population of their ideal community to remain stationary. The means to this end are different in each case. Child exposure and abortion, which Plato proposed as something obvious, never entered More's head, who recommended a socialistic colonial and emigration policy, which was in stark contradiction to the policy of his time. He did not desire the subjugation and exploitation of the natives, but their admission into the new polity as citizens with equal rights and their participation in the higher mode of production brought to them by the colonists.

He was, however, as much constrained as Plato to assume that the population should remain at a given level, as both of them based their commonwealths on husbandry and handicraft. These forms of production are conservative, they develop the productive power of labour but slowly and imperceptibly, frequently ossifying when they reach a certain level. Once the whole of the fertile soil of a country is occupied, any substantial increase in the population is impossible on the basis of peasant agriculture without inflicting harm on the community.

The population question assumes another shape when large-scale undertakings in industry and agriculture arise. This form of production invokes the aid of science, by whose tireless researches and discoveries it is constantly revolutionised. The productivity of labour is continuously increased, and a certain steady growth of the population is thereby rendered possible. The productivity of labour will increase with the development of the division of labour within society, with the restriction of each separate undertaking to the manufacture of a specific article upon a wholesale scale. The steady growth of this mass production and of the possibility of marketing these products is a preliminary condition for the progress of the mode of production under modern technical conditions. Such a growth is possible by raising the standard of life, and thus increasing individual consumption, by increasing the number of consumers, either by extending the area of the market or by augmenting the population.

Under certain circumstances it may be necessary to regulate the pace of this growth. A limitation of the population to a specific number, as More advocated, and was obliged to advocate, is, however, contrary to the modern mode of production, as it is to modern Socialism.

CHAPTER IV

POLITICS, SCIENCE, AND RELIGION IN UTOPIA

1. *Politics.*

THE mode of production, the household, the family, and marriage are the most important spheres in which a particular communistic system can display its characteristic features. The political and ideological superstructure seems to us of less importance. There is not much to be said about politics generally in a communistic community. And as regards the ideas which will prevail therein, it must be admitted that it is easier to imagine institutions which deviate from ours than ideas and mental qualities. The religious and philosophical discussions in *Utopia* are remarkably daring for the time, and throw a vivid light on More. But whereas his economic assumptions are often revolutionary even for to-day, his philosophy, where it is not obsolete, has become commonplace, and might be endorsed by the most timid Liberal. Consequently, the philosophy and religion of *Utopia* have mostly interested our Liberal historians, who have devoted long treatises to this subject, while dismissing the communism with a few phrases as vain imaginings. The philosophy and religion of *Utopia* constitute an important corroboration of More's literary and scientific attitude, as discussed by us in a previous chapter, but they have no organic connection with the communism of his ideal commonwealth.

We shall therefore only repeat what is most important in the long discussions upon these subjects contained in *Utopia* and limit our criticism to what is most necessary to be said.

First let us see how More elaborates the political constitution of Utopia. "Thirty families choose every year a magistrate, who was anciently called the Syphogrant, but is now called the Philarch; and over every ten Syphogrants, with the families subject to them, there is another magistrate, who was anciently called the Tranibor, but of late the Archphilarch. All the Syphogrants, who are in number 200, choose the Prince out of a list of four, who are named by the people of the four divisions of the city; but they take an oath, before they proceed to an election, that they will choose him whom they think most fit for the office. They give their voices secretly, so that it is not known for whom everyone gives his suffrage. The Prince is for life, unless he is removed upon suspicion of some design to enslave the people. The Tranibors are new chosen every year, but yet they are for the most part continued. All their other magistrates are only annual. The Tranibors meet every third day, and oftener if necessary, and consult with the Prince, either concerning the affairs of the State in general, or such private differences as may arise sometimes among the people; though that falls out but seldom. There are always two Syphogrants called into the council-chamber, and these are changed every day. It is a fundamental rule of their government, that no conclusion can be made in anything that relates to the public, till it has been first debated three several days in their council. It is death for any to meet and consult concerning the State, unless it be either in their ordinary council, or in the assembly of the whole body of the people.

"These things have been so provided among them, that

the Prince and the Tranibors may not conspire together to change the government, and enslave the people; and therefore when anything of great importance is set on foot, it is sent to the Syphogrants; who after they have communicated it to the families that belong to their divisions, and have considered it among themselves, make report to the Senate; and upon great occasions, the matter is referred to the council of the whole island. . . ."

Each town sends annually three of its wisest elders to Amaurot, the Capital, to conduct the public business of the island. As we know, the function of this Senate is to compile statistics of the requirements and produce of every town, and to adjust superfluities and shortages.

"The chief, and almost the only, business " of these officials, " is to take care that no man may live idle, but that every one may follow his trade diligently."

We read in another place: " If any man aspires to any office he is sure never to compass it. They all live easily together, for none of the magistrates are either insolent or cruel to the people; they affect rather to be called fathers, and, by being really so, they well deserve the name; and the people pay them all the marks of honour the more freely because none are exacted from them. The Prince himself has no distinction, either of garments or of a crown; but is only distinguished by a sheaf of corn carried before him; as the High Priest is also known by his being preceded by a person carrying a wax light.

" They have but few laws, and such is their constitution that they need not many. They very much condemn other nations whose laws, together with the commentaries on them, swell up to so many volumes."

The foreign political relations of the Utopians are as simple as their internal relations. They do not make treaties with foreign peoples, as they know that such treaties are kept only so long as they are advantageous. They rely upon themselves and upon the economic dependence of neighbours upon them.

"They detest war as a very brutal thing, and which, to the reproach of human nature, is more practised by men than by any sort of beasts. They, in opposition to the sentiments of almost all other nations, think that there is nothing more inglorious than that glory that is gained by war; and therefore, though they accustom themselves daily to military exercises and the discipline of war, in which not only their men, but their women likewise, are trained up, that, in cases of necessity, they may not be quite useless, yet they do not rashly engage in war, unless it be either to defend themselves or their friends from any unjust aggressors, or, out of good-nature or in compassion, assist an oppressed nation in shaking off the yoke of tyranny. . . ." They regard it as a just cause for war when "one neighbour makes an inroad on another by public order, and carries away the spoils, but also when the merchants of one country are oppressed in another, either under pretence of some unjust laws, or by the perverse wresting of good ones."

His uncommonly finely drawn discussions upon war, of which we have only given the commencement, are mostly nothing more than scorching satire upon the war spirit of his time, in which the Swiss, who appear under the name of Zapolets, are specially singled out. These discussions are based on the assumption that his communistic commonwealth is surrounded by States at the same level of civilisation, while possessing social and political institutions opposed to those of Utopia. More had scarcely a glimmering of the international solidarity of modern Socialism, which regards the social transformation to which he aspired as the necessary product of the capitalist mode of production, and therefore assumes that it will extend to all the countries in which this mode of production prevails.

The discussions upon the internal political organisation of Utopia are more closely related to communism than the discussions upon war. It is an entirely democratic community, in which the functions of the authorities, apart from composing disputes, consist almost exclusively in the direction of labour. More stands here on the ground of modern Socialism, in predicting that with the abolition of class antagonisms, the political functions will dwindle, and the community will be transformed from a political State into a co-operative commonwealth.

It is characteristic of More that he could not imagine such a community without a prince. It is true the latter has nothing to do except to avoid coming under suspicion of striving for absolute power.

2. *Science.*

Let us now consider the place which Science occupies in Utopia: " It is ordinary to have public lectures every morning before daybreak, at which none are obliged to appear but those who are marked out for literature; yet a great many, both men and women, of all ranks, go to hear lectures of one sort or another, according to their inclinations."

These few lines contain one of the most important principles of modern Socialism: the abolition of the privilege of science and literature for a caste. Science and literature are rendered equally accessible to all citizens of the commonwealth, women as well as men, and one of the most important, perhaps the chief, aim of the commonwealth consists in allowing everybody to share in intellectual labour. " The chief end of the constitution," it is stated in *Utopia*, " is to regulate labour by the necessities of the public, and to allow the people as much time as is necessary for the improvement of their minds, in which they think the happiness of life consists."

This is quite a modern idea which formed no part of primitive or of Platonic communism. Primitive man was debarred from the enjoyment of scientific activity.

The impulse to such activity would arise, on the one hand, when the elements of society were caught up in a more rapid development, when hostile classes came into existence, when social changes entered upon a development independent of the human will, and social struggles provoked men to reflection upon their meaning, when mankind received a history; on the other hand, only when man was freed from the umbilical cord of nature, when nature confronted him as something objective. Both foundations of the need for scientific research developed with sufficient strength only in the towns; and there also developed simultaneously the conditions which made scientific research possible, the creation of a class, which, freed from the necessity of physical labour, could apply itself wholly to intellectual activity.

Labour and science in the days of Antiquity seemed to be two incompatible things. Consequently, even in the Platonic Republic science is the privilege of the ruling and exploiting class.

More's communism, resting as it does on equal obligation to work, and therefore on universal equality, must also, like primitive communism, admit the equal right of all to share in enjoyment. This must be the case all the more with the greatest and most lasting of enjoyments, which only appeared with the decay of primitive communism, the enjoyment of mental labour. Upon this More must perforce lay special stress as a Humanist, for a life without intellectual activity did not seem worth living. And as the conditions for the liberation of all citizens from mind-killing physical work without restricting wants did not yet exist, More preferred the latter alternative. We have already discussed this point, and know that More was compelled by the technical backwardness of his age to create two classes, insignificant in numbers it is true, whose existence contradicts the principles of *Utopia*: a class of scholars, freed from the general obligation to work, and a class of slaves, debarred from intellectual activity. It must, however, be emphasised that the scholars do not enjoy any material advantages over the other citizens. And More did not consider it necessary to raise this question.

It must not be inferred from the stress which More lays on the enjoyment of intellectual labour that he despises sensuous enjoyments. The common suppers in Utopia are not marked by ascetic simplicity.

They eat well, there is no lack of sweetmeats, music and scents stimulate the senses. Moreover, the Utopians' outlook on life is serene and joyous.

We find this set out in a lengthy excursus which forms the conclusion of the chapter on "The Travels of the Utopians." This excursus is very important for the light it throws upon the position of science in Utopia; the contempt shown for the purely speculative sciences which played so great a part in More's time, and the respect shown for the natural sciences, are especially noteworthy. We cannot better conclude our discussion of science in Utopia than by citing a few passages from this chapter.

" These and such like notions has that people imbibed, partly from their education, being bred in a country whose customs and laws are opposite to all such foolish maxims, and partly from their learning and studies; for though there are but few in any town that are so wholly excused from labour as to give themselves entirely up

to their studies, these being only such persons as discover
from their childhood an extraordinary capacity and
disposition for letters; yet their children, and a great part
of the nation, both men and women, are taught to spend
those hours in which they are not obliged to work in reading: and this they do through the whole progress of life.
They have all their learning in their own tongue. . . .
They had made the same discoveries as the Greeks, both
in music, logic, arithmetic, and geometry. Yet they far
exceed our modern logicians; for they have never yet
fallen upon the barbarous niceties that our youth are
forced to learn in those trifling logical schools that are
among us; they are so far from minding chimeras, and
fantastical images made in the mind, that none of them
could comprehend what we meant when we talked to them
of a man in the abstract, as common to all men in particular (so that though we spoke of him as a thing that we
could point at with our fingers, yet none of them could
perceive him), and yet distinct from every one, as if he
were some monstrous Colossus or giant. Yet for all this
ignorance of these empty notions, they knew astronomy,
and were perfectly acquainted with the motions of the
heavenly bodies, and have many instruments, well contrived and divided, by which they very accurately com-
pute the course and positions of the sun, moon, and stars.
But for the cheat, of divining by the stars by their opposi-
tions or conjunctions, it has not so much as entered
into their thoughts. They have a particular sagacity,
founded upon much observation, in judging of the weather,
by which they know when they may look for rain, wind,
or other alterations in the air; but as to the philosophy
of these things, the causes of the saltness of the sea, of its
ebbing and flowing, and of the origin and nature both of
the heavens and the earth; they dispute of them, partly
as our ancient philosophers have done, and partly upon

some new hypothesis, in which, as they differ from them, so they do not in all things agree among themselves.

" As to moral philosophy, they have the same disputes among them as we have here: they examine what are properly good both for the body and the mind, and whether any outward thing can be called truly good, or if that term belong only to the endowments of the soul. They enquire likewise into the nature of virtue and pleasure; but their chief dispute is concerning the happiness of a man, and wherein it consists ? Whether in some one thing, or in a great many ? They seem, indeed, more inclinable to that opinion that places, if not the whole, yet the chief part of a man's happiness in pleasure; and, what may seem more strange, they make use of arguments even from religion, notwithstanding its severity and roughness, for the support of that opinion so indulgent to pleasure.

" They define virtue thus, that it is a living according to Nature, and think that we are made by God for that end; they believe that a man then follows the dictates of Nature when he pursues or avoids things according to the direction of reason; they say that the first dictate of reason is the kindling in us a love and reverence for the Divine Majesty, to whom we owe both all that we have, and all that we can ever hope for. In the next place, reason directs us to keep our minds as free from passion and as cheerful as we can, and that we should consider ourselves as bound by the ties of good-nature and humanity to use our utmost endeavours to help forward the happiness of all other persons. . . .

" But of all pleasures, they esteem those to be most valuable that lie in the mind; the chief of which arises out of true virtue, and the witness of a good conscience. They account health the chief pleasure that belongs to the body; for they think that the pleasure of eating and drinking, and all the other delights of sense, are only so far desirable as they give or maintain health. . . .   They think, therefore, none of those pleasures are to be valued any further than as they are necessary; yet they rejoice in them, and with due gratitude acknowledge the tenderness of the great Author of Nature, who has planted in us appetites, by which those things that are necessary for our preservation are likewise made pleasant to us."

3. *Religion.*

Let us turn from the Pagan rather than Christian philosophy to the religious institutions of the Utopians.

" There are several sorts of religions, not only in different parts of the island, but even in every town; some worshipping the sun, others the moon, or one of the planets; some worship such men as have been eminent in former times for virtue, or glory, not only as ordinary deities, but as the supreme God: yet the greater and wiser sort of them worship none of these, but adore one eternal, invisible, infinite, and incomprehensible Deity; as a Being that is far above all our apprehensions, that is spread over the whole universe, not by His bulk, but by His power and virtue; Him they call the Father of All. . . .   And indeed, though they differ concerning other things, yet all agree in this, that they think there is one supreme Being that made and governs the world, whom they call in the language of their country Mithras. . . .   One of their most ancient laws is that no man ought to be punished for his religion.   At the first constitution of their government, Utopus having understood that before his coming among them the old inhabitants had been engaged in great quarrels concerning religion, by which they were so divided among themselves, that he found it an easy thing to conquer them, since, instead of uniting their forces against him, every different party in religion fought by themselves; after he had subdued them, he made a law that every man might be of what religion he pleased, and might endeavour to draw others to it by the force of argument, and by amicable and modest ways, but without bitterness against those of other opinions; and such as did otherwise were to be condemned to banishment or slavery.

" This law was made by Utopus, not only for preserving the public peace which he saw suffered much by daily contentions and irreconcilable heats, but because he thought the interest of religion itself required it. He judged it not fit to determine anything rashly, and seemed to doubt whether those different forms of religion might not all come from God, who might inspire men in a different manner, and be pleased with this variety; he therefore thought it indecent and foolish for any man to threaten and terrify another to make him believe what did not appear to him to be true. And supposing that only one religion was really true, and the rest false, he imagined that the native force of truth would at last break forth and shine bright, if supported only by the strength of argument, and attended to with a gentle and unprejudiced mind; while, on the other hand, if such debates were carried on with violence and tumults, as the most wicked are always the most obstinate, so the best and most holy religion might be choked with superstition, as corn is with briars and thorns; he therefore left men wholly to their liberty, that they might be free to believe as they should see cause; only he made a solemn and severe law against such as should so far degenerate from the dignity of human nature as to think that our souls died with our bodies, or that the world was governed by chance, without a wise overruling Providence. . . . They never raise any that hold these maxims, either to honours or offices, nor employ them in any public trust, but despise them, as men of base and sordid minds; yet they do not punish them, because they lay this down as a maxim that a man cannot make himself believe anything he pleases; nor do they drive any to dissemble their thoughts by threatenings, so that men are not tempted to lie or disguise their opinions. They take care indeed to prevent their disputing in defence of these opinions, especially before the common people; but they suffer, and even encourage them to dispute concerning them in private with their priests and other grave men, being confident that they will be cured of those mad opinions by having reason laid before them."

These discussions, so far as they relate to the toleration of all creeds, are more suggestive of the age of "Enlightenment" than of the Reformation, more in harmony with the age in which *Nathan the Wise* was written than the age in which Calvin burnt Servetus, immediately before the bloodiest wars of religion that the world has ever seen, and they seem to us all the more generous as not coming from an unbeliever, who actually stood above religions, but from a profoundly religious spirit, a man who found in religion the sole medium which his age offered for giving expression to his enthusiastic love of mankind, for whom irreligiosity was synonymous with lack of common sense. The Materialism of the sixteenth century arose, in fact, not among the exploited, but among the exploiting classes. Those who disbelieved in God and immortality were Popes and cardinals, princes and courtiers; their contempt for religion was concomitant with their contempt for the people. This must be borne in mind, in order to understand why More excluded Materialists as common egoists from the political administration.

While More was akin to the eighteenth century in his tolerance, he anticipated the Reformation in the organisation of his ideal Church.

" Their priests are men of eminent piety, and therefore they are but few, for there are only thirteen in every town, one for every temple. . . . They are chosen by the people as the other magistrates are, by suffrages given in secret, for preventing of factions; and when they are chosen they are consecrated by the college of priests. The care of all sacred things, the worship of God, and an inspection into the manners of the people, are committed to them. It is a reproach to a man to be sent for by any of them, or for them to speak to him in secret, for that always gives some suspicion. All that is incumbent on them is only to exhort and admonish the people; for the power of correcting and punishing ill men belongs wholly to the Prince and to the other magistrates. . . . The education of youth belongs to the priests, yet they do not take so much care of instructing them in letters as in forming their minds and manners aright; they use all possible methods to infuse very early into the tender and flexible minds of children such opinions as are both good in themselves and will be useful to their country. For when deep impressions of these things are made at that age, they follow men through the whole course of their lives, and conduce much to preserve the peace of the government, which suffers by nothing more than by vices that rise out of ill opinions. The wives of their priests are the most extraordinary women of the whole country; sometimes the women themselves are made priests, though that falls out but seldom, nor are any but ancient widows chosen into that order.

"Though there are many different forms of religion among them, yet all these, how various soever, agree in the main point, which is the worshipping the Divine Essence; and therefore there is nothing to be seen or heard in their temples in which the several persuasions among them may not agree; for every sect performs those rites that are peculiar to it, in their private houses, nor is there anything in the public worship that contradicts the particular ways of those different sects. There are no images of God in their temples, so that every one may represent Him to their thoughts, according to the way of his religion. . . .

" The last day of the month, and of the year, is a festival . . . before they go to the temple, both wives and children fall on their knees before their husbands or parents, and confess everything in which they have either erred or failed in their duty, and beg pardon for it. Thus all little discontents in families are removed, that they may offer up their devotions with a pure and serene mind."

What an advance this Utopian Church marks upon Lutheranism and even Calvinism ! It agrees with both in the abolition of aural confession, of priestly celibacy, of the worship of images, and with Calvinism in providing for the election of the priests by the people. But More goes further. He abolishes, for instance, the coercive powers of the priesthood, and admits women to the priesthood. He does not shrink from recommending suicide to incurable invalids. In the common divine service of all creeds and the relegation of special services to the home, More is in advance of every Church of his age. This is in the language of the sixteenth century the same principle that modern Socialism has adopted, in declaring religion to be a private matter.

We see how revolutionary *Utopia* was: revolutionary not only in reference to a remote future, but also in relation to the burning questions of its time. It attacks not only private property, not only the policy of princes, not only the ignorance and laziness of the monks, but even the doctrines of religion.

CHAPTER V

THE AIM OF "UTOPIA"

AFTER More has given in detail the picture of an ideal society which forms the exact opposite of the society of his time, at the conclusion of *Utopia* he once more flings down the gauntlet in a vehement apostrophe.

Modern Socialism has hardly emitted a sharper criticism of society than is contained in the sentences with which Hythloday concludes his account of the Utopians.

"Thus have I described to you, as particularly as I could, the constitution of that commonwealth, which I do not only think the best in the world, but indeed the only commonwealth that truly deserves that name. In all other places it is visible, that while people talk of a commonwealth every man seeks his own wealth; but there, where no man has any property, all men zealously pursue the good of the public; and, indeed, it is no wonder to see men act so differently; for in other commonwealths every man knows that unless he provides for himself, how flourishing soever the commonwealth may be, he must die of hunger; so that he sees the necessity of preferring his own concerns to the public; but in Utopia, where every man has a right to everything, they all know that if care is taken to keep the public stores full, no private man can want anything; for among them there is no unequal distribution, so that no man is poor, none in necessity, and though no man has anything, yet they are all rich; for what can make a man so rich as to lead a serene and cheerful life, free from anxieties; neither apprehending want himself, nor vexed with the endless complaints of his wife ?   He is not afraid of the misery of his children, nor is he contriving how to raise a portion for his daughters, but is secure in this, that both he and his wife, his children and grandchildren, to as many generations as he can fancy, will all live both plentifully and happily; since among them there is no less care taken of those who were once engaged in labour, but grow afterwards unable to follow it, than there is elsewhere of those that continue still employed.   I would gladly hear any man compare the justice that is among them with that of all other nations; among whom, may I perish, if I see anything that looks either like justice or equity: for what justice is there in this, that a nobleman, a goldsmith, a banker, or any other man, that either does nothing at all, or at best is employed in things that are of no use to the public, should live in great luxury and splendour, upon what is so ill acquired; and a mean man, a carter, a smith, or a ploughman, that works harder even than the beasts them- selves, and is employed in labours so necessary, that no commonwealth could hold out a year without them, can only earn so poor a livelihood, and must lead so miserable a life, that the condition of the beasts is much better than theirs ?   For as the beasts do not work so constantly, so they feed almost as well, and with more pleasure; and have no anxiety about what is to come, whilst these men are depressed by a barren and fruitless employment, and tormented with the apprehensions of want in their old age; since that which they get by their daily labour does but maintain them at present, and is consumed as fast as it comes in, there is no overplus left to lay up for old age.

" Is not that government both unjust and ungrateful, that is so prodigal of its favours to those that are called gentlemen, or goldsmiths, or such others who are idle, or live either by flattery, or by contriving the arts of vain pleasure; and on the other hand, takes no care of those of a meaner sort, such as ploughmen, colliers, and smiths, without whom it could not subsist ? But after the public has reaped all the advantage of their service, and they come to be oppressed with age, sickness, and want, all their labours and the good they have done is forgotten; and all the recompense given them is that they are left to die in great misery. The richer sort are often endeavouring to bring the hire of labourers lower, not only by their fraudulent practices, but by the laws which they procure to be made to that effect; so that though it is a thing most unjust in itself, to give such small rewards to those who deserve so well of the public, yet they have given those hardships the name and colour of justice, by procuring laws to be made for regulating them.

" Therefore I must say that, as I hope for mercy, I can have no other notion of all the other governments that I see or know, than that they are a conspiracy of the rich, who on pretence of managing the public only pursue their private ends, and devise all the ways and arts they can find out; first, that they may, without danger, preserve all that that they have so ill acquired, and then that they may engage the poor to toil and labour for them at as low rates as possible, and oppress them as much as they pleasure. And if they can but prevail to get these contrivances established by the show of public authority, which is considered as the representative of the whole people, then they are accounted laws. Yet these wicked men after they have, by a most insatiable covetousness, divided that among themselves with which all the rest might have been well supplied, are far from that happiness that is enjoyed among the Utopians; for the use as well as the desire of money being extinguished, much anxiety and great occasions of mischief is cut off with it.   And who does not see that the frauds, thefts, robberies, quarrels, tumults, contentions, seditions, murders, treacheries, and witchcrafts, which are indeed rather punished than restrained by the severities of law, would all fall off, if money were not any more valued by the world ?   Men's fears, solicitudes, cares, labours, and watchings, would all perish in the same moment with the value of money; even poverty itself, for the relief of which money seems most necessary, would fall."

Compared with this bold criticism, which attacks society at its roots, how limited does not the much be-lauded action of Luther appear, who commenced a year after the appearance of *Utopia* to preach against, not indulgences themselves, but the abuse of indulgences, and was impelled to take further steps not by a logical process going on in his mind, but by the logic of facts !   And yet while the whole might of Rome was eventually summoned against the man who attacked the abuse of indulgences, without purposing to make any change in the ecclesiastical organisation, no molestation was offered to the man whose doctrines tended to sap the very foundations of society; and the advocate of a Church who was as uncatholic, and in many respects even unchristian, as any one of the reformed churches, became a martyr of the Catholic religion.

Strange as this difference in treatment appears, there was good reason for it.   Luther addressed himself to the masses; he expressed the interests of powerful classes and parties.   More, with his aspirations, stood alone; he addressed only a small circle of scholars, the people did not understand him and he did not desire to be understood by the people.   He therefore wrote his *Utopia* in Latin, and concealed his thoughts in the garment of satire, which to be sure permitted him greater freedom in the expression of his opinions.

This brings us to the last question which remains to be answered: What did More aim at in his *Utopia*?

We know that some regard it merely as an imitation of the Platonic Republic, while others declare it to be an idle fantasy.

We believe, however, that we have sufficiently shown that More's Communism differs essentially from that of Plato, and instead of being " a splendid fruit of the study of antiquity," as Rudhart would have us believe in his *Thomas Morus*, it is the product of the social evils and incipient economic tendencies of the Renascence; and that it is based on living actualities, and not on antiquarian book wisdom.

The idea that it was written as a jest may be dismissed. It was taken very seriously by More's contemporaries. Budæus, for example, wrote to Lupsetus: "We are greatly indebted to Thomas More for his *Utopia*, in which he holds up to the world a model of social felicity. Our age and our posterity will regard this exposition as a source of excellent doctrines and useful ordinances, from which States will construct their institutions." Numerous other contemporaries of More express themselves in a similar sense, scholars and statesmen like Johannes Paludanus, Paulus Jonius and Hieronymus Buslidianus. Stapleton has collected a number of pronouncements upon *Utopia* all of which are couched in the terms of the above quotation. All saw in *Utopia* a book which gives directions to rulers how to govern their States.

And this was quite in accordance with the trend of that time. In the view then prevailing, everything was possible to a prince, and to those who gained the support of a prince. More's age was marked by a plethora of directions to princes. Macchiavelli's *Prince* and Erasmus' *Manual for Christian Princes* were composed at the same time as *Utopia*, and we have not the slightest reason for doubting that the aim of the latter was the same as the aim of the former: to show princes how they should govern.

And *Utopia* even pursued the special object of influencing the government and constitution of England. This is not only shown very distinctly in the first book, but Erasmus, who ought to have known it, relates this fact in his well-known letter to Hutten: "He published his *Utopia* for the purpose of showing, what are the things that occasion mischief in commonwealths; having the English Constitution especially in view."

The island of Utopia is, in fact, England. More designed to show how England would look, and what shape her relations with abroad would assume, if she were communistically organised.

The analogy may be traced with exactitude: The island is separated from the Continent only by a channel 21 miles wide. The description of the capital, Amaurot, is a true description of London. Stow, in his *Survey of London*, vol. ii., p. 458, finds a perfect correspondence between the two towns.

Historians and economists who are perplexed by *Utopia* perceive in this name a subtle hint by More that he himself regarded his communism as an impracticable dream.

In all the discussions about the Utopians there is only one element of a fantastic nature, and that is not the goal that was aimed at, but the ways and means of achieving it. More saw only one force which could carry communism into effect, and this he mistrusted. He has shown us in his *Utopia* in what manner he conceived that communism would be enforced. A prince named Utopus conquered the country, and impressed on it the stamp of his mind; all institutions in Utopia are to be traced to him. He thought out the general plan of the commonwealth and then put it into execution.

In this way More conceived the realisation of his ideals: he was the father of Utopian Socialism, which was rightly named after his *Utopia*. The latter is Utopian less on account of the impracticability of its aims than on account of the inadequacy of the means at its disposal for their achievement.

We know that More could not help being an Utopist. As yet there was no party, no class to champion Socialism; the decisive political power, on which the State seemed to depend, were the princes, then a young, and in a sense a revolutionary element, without defined traditions: why should not one of them be converted to Communism? If such a prince desired, he could enforce Communism. If no prince so desired, the poverty of the people was unalterable. So thought More, and from this standpoint he was impelled to make an attempt to convert a prince. But he was by no means deceived as to the hopelessness of his task. He knew the princes of his time too well.

He concludes *Utopia* with the following words, after inserting a saving clause that he did not agree with all that Hythloday had related: "However, there are many things in the commonwealth of Utopia that I rather wish, than hope, to see followed in our governments."

In this conclusion lies the whole tragedy of More's fate, the whole tragedy of a genius who divines the problems of his age before the material conditions exist for their solution; the whole tragedy of a character who feels obliged to grapple with the solution of the problems which the age has presented, to champion the rights of the oppressed against the arrogance of the ruling classes, even when he stands alone and his efforts have no prospect of success.

More proved the grandeur of his character when he ascended the scaffold because he would not sacrifice his conviction to a princely caprice. It was already recognised by his contemporaries, who could not, however, grasp the magnitude of his genius, much as they praised it. Only in modern times, with the rise of scientific Socialism, has it become possible to do full justice to More the Socialist. Only since the second half of the nineteenth century have the aims of Socialism as a historic phenomenon been so obvious as to render it possible to separate the essential from the unessential, the permanent from the transitory in the beginnings of the Socialist Movement. Only with this has it become possible to perceive what in *Utopia* is the fantastic amusement of an idle hour, what is the echo of the past, what is a presentiment of the future, and what is historical fact.

And nothing speaks more eloquently for the greatness of the man, nothing shows more distinctly how he towered above his contemporaries, than that it required more than three centuries before the conditions existed which enable us to perceive that he set himself aims which are not the idle dreaming of a leisure hour, but the result of a profound insight into the essentials of the economic tendencies of his age. Although *Utopia* is more than four hundred years old, the ideals of More are not vanquished, but still lie before striving mankind.

BILLING AND SONS, LTD., GUILDFORD AND ESHER

CPSIA information can be obtained
at www.ICGtesting.com
Printed in the USA
BVHW091243120919
558269BV00004B/598/P